Household Solutions 2

with Kitchen Secrets

1500 QUICK FIXES

Hundred of Remedies, Tips & Everyday Kitchen Secrets

Dedicated to the best household secret of all, family.

Reena Nerbas

Household Solutions 2 with Kitchen Secrets
by Reena Nerbas

First Printing – May 2007

Published by Publishing Solutions, a division of PrintWest Communications Ltd.

NOTICE: The solutions and substitutions described in this publication have not been tested by Publishing Solutions. Publishing Solutions gives no warranty as to the useful-ness, or as to the safety, of the suggestions which follow. Any problems arising from the use of these solutions and substitutions are the responsibility of the user. Use of these recommendations is solely the decision of the reader. Every user assumes all risks of injury or damage to whatsoever kind which may result from the implementation of any and all suggestions herein. Readers are warned that the combination of solutions and substitutions involving the use of chemical agents may be dangerous. This book would not have been possible without the solutions from many generous contributors. Thank you to all who sent in tips and hints!

Library and Archives Canada Cataloguing in Publication

Nerbas, Reena, 1967-

Household solutions 2 with kitchen secrets : 1500 quick fixes / by Reena Nerbas.

     Includes index.

     ISBN: 978-1-897010-39-6

1. Home economics – Miscellanea. I. Title.

TX158.N472 2007   640'.41   C2007-902620-6

Cover and page design by Brian Danchuk, Brian Danchuk Design, Regina
Cover photo by Inscho & Lindsey's Photography, Steinbach, MB
Page formatting and Index by Iona Glabus

Designed, Printed and Produced in Canada by:
Centax Books, a Division of PrintWest Communications Ltd.
Publishing Co-ordinator: Iona Glabus
1150 Eighth Avenue, Regina, Saskatchewan, Canada   S4R 1C9
(306) 525-2304   FAX: (306) 757-2439
centax@printwest.com   www.centaxbooks.com

Introduction

From my home to yours ... You asked for it and here it is, brand new tips, secrets and hints from around the world! With every interview, whether it be radio, television or in person, I continue to learn and the mail continues to pour in with advice about: cleaning, cooking, health and safety, chemicals in our world, food storage and so much more. Just when I think that household secrets might soon be exhausted, another 20 find their way to my computer; there seems to be no end. It is my great privilege to present to you, *Household Solutions 2 with Kitchen Secrets!*

Ever notice that many household cleaners do not have an ingredients label? Also, many labels are incomplete and misleading. Of more than 75,000 chemicals registered to date, only a handful have been thoroughly tested for safety. This includes baby-wipes, shampoos, cleaners and cosmetics, just to name a few. Companies are able to withhold information about their products and the recipes that they are manufacturing because of a law known as "Trade Secrets" that evolved in England during the Industrial Revolution. Historically, trade secrets have been with us since ancient times in the form of keeping advanced military technology from one's enemies and, in more recent times, in keeping Industrial Revolution era technology secret.

This leaves the general public living in a world of hidden information about products that are sold every second of every day. Inundated with advertisements and advice about which cosmetics to buy and what cleans the best, we head to the store making decisions about products that we feel are best for our families, only to find out months later that they have been proven harmful. Advertisers advise us on purchasing anti-bacterial agents that will kill all of the bacteria in our homes but fail to mention that bacteria is necessary for human life, see page 78.

We do have choices. We can purchase products that we know and trust and that have been successfully used for centuries. Why do so few people know about borax, washing soda, vinegar and many other all around products that I consider "Household Superstars"? Household Superstars go above and beyond their intended uses and are less expensive, often safer and more effective, than 21st Century products. Some of these products have been around for 4,000 years.

Solutions 2

Household Solutions 1 with Substitutions (previously published under the title of *Household Solutions & Substitutions*) is a National Best Seller because the ideas included are easy to use and bring us back to basics. It includes ideas and tricks from around the world, hints that our grandparents not only used but lived by. *Household Solutions 2 with Kitchen Secrets* is a book packed with solutions to everyday problems.

"*Solutions* is the kind of book everyone needs to keep close at hand. With answers for nearly every conceivable minor household emergency, these hints and tips cover everything from stain removal to reducing heating bills. Written in an engaging, personable style, this book is, much like Reena herself, fun and informative. Whenever someone asks me to suggest a book as a gift-giving idea, I immediately point them to *Solutions*."
  – Keith Edmunds, Pennywise Books, Brandon MB

"Reena Nerbas is to domestic affairs what Bill Gates is to computers. No responsible person should keep house without her advice."
  – Andrew Matte, Editor, *Regina Sun*

"Thank you so much Reena, for the reminder about washing soda, my husband's tuxedo shirt was lightly splattered at a banquet and I put some washing soda in a bowl with the required amount of water; spooned it onto the affected areas, waited, rubbed lightly, then hung the shirt in the shower and rinsed lightly. I think you just saved me a trip to the cleaners, time and money. What a fantastic hint!"
  – Betty Eskdale, Regina, Saskatchewan

Life just got easier!

Acknowledgements

Special thanks to: Margo Embury, Dan Marce, Iona Glabus, Tracy Wilson and staff at Centax, Wade Nerbas, Jordan Nerbas, Kristi Nerbas, Kyah Nerbas, Austin Nerbas, Margret Malaviya, Rekha Malaviya, Sharon Nerbas, Garry Nerbas, Glenda Armstrong, Esther Bast and Sheila Kolesar.

Also, special thanks to Kelly Taylor and the *Winnipeg Free Press*, who first printed selected "Solutions" lists, and Bonnie Thompson who first printed selected lists in *Grainews* and *The Manitoba Cooperator*.

Reena's Q & A on Household Survival

Question: What can you do to prevent your bathroom sink from plugging up and emitting a foul odor?

Answer: Once a week pour ¼ cup (60 mL) baking soda (helps dissolve soap scum and grease) down the drain, followed by ½ cup (125 mL) vinegar (burns away mineral deposits and scale). The solution will fizz. Wait 20 minutes and pour 1 gallon (4 L) boiling water down the drain.

Question: Why is it a good idea to load each type of cutlery into its own compartment in the dishwasher?

Answer: It will save you time during the unloading process.

Question: Your scissors dull, what should you do?

Answer: Cut S.O.S pads in half, this will sharpen the blades. Cutting through aluminum foil works also.

Question: True or False: For a perfectly colored piecrust, combine 1 egg white and 1 tsp. (5 mL) milk in a bowl. Brush over piecrust during the last 10 minutes of baking.

Answer: True

Question: When laundering protein stains, e.g., egg, dairy, blood, etc., should you use hot or cold water?

Answer: Cold water, hot water will set the stain.

Question: Why is milk effective in removing ballpoint ink and red juice stains?

Answer: The enzymes that turn milk sour are the same enzymes that break down stains and make them disappear.

Question: When doubling a recipe for cookies, do you …
  A   Double the amount of salt.
  B   Triple the amount of salt.
  C   Use the same amount of salt that the recipe originally called for.

Answer:

Table of Contents

Solutions

Table of Contents

Kitchen Secrets

Household Superstars and Outstanding Cleaning Recipes

To be considered a household superstar, a product must have effective uses beyond its original intention. Meet the best of the best!

- **Acetone, Denatured Alcohol, Petroleum Distillates** (such as kerosene, mineral spirits, dry cleaning fluids, etc.) and **Turpentine**: Use to remove greasy soil, or stains that will not dissolve in water; or use for cleaning surfaces that would be damaged by water. Some remove waxes, wood finishes, and oil-base paint. They are used in most wood polishes and waxes, in spot removers, some rug cleaners, degreasers, and in some all-purpose household cleaners. **Caution: Most are flammable: some will explode.** Wear rubber gloves, keep off skin and out of eyes, and do not breathe fumes excessively. Don't wear contact lenses when using solvents, don't drink alcohol during or after use, and don't use when pregnant. Read label directions and follow exactly. **Note:** Denatured Alcohol is stronger than rubbing alcohol.

 All-Purpose Cleaner Recipe: In a spray bottle, combine 2 cups (500 mL) rubbing alcohol, ½ cup (125 mL) ammonia, 1 tsp. (5 mL) Dawn dish soap and enough water to fill the bottle. Spray, wipe and rinse.

 Aluminum Cookware Cleaner: Fill the pot half full with water; add 2 tbsp. (30 mL) cream of tartar and half pot of water. Bring solution to a simmer for 15 minutes. Rinse and dry.

 Ammonia: Removes stains on bakeware, carpet and fabric. **Caution:** Do not breath in fumes. **Smoke Smell on Walls**: In a spray bottle, mix 1 gallon (4 L) water with ½ cup (125 mL) ammonia, ¼ cup (60 mL) vinegar and ¼ cup (60 mL) washing soda. Rinse well.

 Automatic Dishwasher Detergent: Works like bleach. Clean vinyl floors with ¼ cup (60 mL) dishwasher detergent and 1 gallon (4 L) boiling water. **Never mix with ammonia.**

- **Baking Soda (Sodium Bicarbonate)**: Originally found in lake sediments and ground water, today all baking soda comes from the mined mineral Trona, in Wyoming. **Uses:** Removes odors, puts out grease fires, keeps ants away, cleans silver, removes coffee stains, cleans ovens (rinse with vinegar), alternative to toothpaste, removes coffee stains in mugs, helps sooth sore throats, tenderizes cabbage, softens fabric, preserves flowers, and the list goes on.

- **Black Fungus on Concrete – Removing**: Spray with 50/50 bleach and water.

- **Borax**: Estimated to be 4,000 years old. In the late 1800s borax was found in Death Valley. It took 20 mules to pull the white powder to the railroad. Hence the name 20 Mule Borax. **Uses**: Laundry whitener, cleans walls, refrigerators, floors, appliances, hats, training pants, toilets, pots and pans, grout cleaner.

- **Brick Cleaner**: Double-strength TSP (trisodium phosphate) and water. Apply to floor or walls. Let sit 5 minutes. Scrub.

- **Club Soda**: In the past soda water was produced in the home by "charging" a refillable seltzer bottle with water and adding sodium bicarbonate, which explains its dynamic cleaning power. **Uses**: Keep a bottle in the house at all times to dab on carpet and fabric stains to clean or at least keep the stain from setting.

- **Cream of Tartar**: The potassium salt or tartaric acid that is left on the inside of wire casks once grapes have fermented. **Uses**: Increase volume to egg whites. Removes bathtub rust, cleans porcelain and whitens fabrics when combined with either hydrogen peroxide or lemon juice.

- **Dandruff Shampoo**: (Head & Shoulders) the main ingredient is Zinc Pyrithione. **Uses**: Cleans lipstick, wax and old bloodstains as well as unknown stains. Never give up on a stain until you have blotted it with dandruff shampoo, wash as usual.

 Denture Tablets: Effervescent tablet for cleaning of dentures. **Uses**: For fingers or fingernails yellowed by smoking, soak fingers in a dish with 1 denture tablet dissolved in 1 cup (250 mL) of water. This also cleans combs, jewelry, teapot or cup stains, vases, will whiten table linens and removes clothing stains. Clean coffee pots by dropping 1 denture tablet into hot water instead of cold.

- **Dawn Dishwashing Liquid**: Made up of a variety of ingredients, which are patented by many commercial companies. **Uses**: Pour on icy areas to prevent slipping. Wipe on mirrors to defog; great spot remover for clothing, furniture and carpets. Make your own dish soap by filling a squeeze bottle with water and Ivory Snow flakes.

 Pre-treating Spot Remover: In a spray bottle, combine 1 cup (250 mL) hydrogen peroxide, 1 cup (250 mL) vinegar, 1 cup (250 mL) water and ½ cup (125 mL) Dawn dish soap. Spray onto fabric stains before tossing the clothing article into the washing machine.

Dye Removal Recipe: When one color of dye has bled into another color, mix ¼ cup (60 mL) dishwasher detergent with 4 cups (1 L) hot water. Let clothes soak for 10 minutes. Rinse immediately in cold water and wash separately. **Note**: Rit makes a dye remover, that will alter overall color appearance and remove stains. Re-dye as desired.

- **Glycerin**: An ingredient found in many soaps and beauty products, it is obtained by saponification of fats and oils. Great at removing ink, grass stains, juice stains, tree sap, mustard, ketchup, etc.

 Grout Cleaner: Use an eraser or ¼ cup (60 mL) washing soda (or baking soda) combined with ¼ cup (60 mL) ammonia and 4 cups (1 L) water. Leave for 10 minutes and rinse. **Note**: Avoid vinegar, it may etch grout.

 High-Gloss Grand Piano Keys: Wipe the keys with 1 tbsp. (15 mL) liquid detergent in 1 quart (1 L) warm water. Dry-polish with a soft cloth.

- **Hydrogen Peroxide**: The only germicidal agent composed of just water and oxygen. Household hydrogen peroxide has a strength of less than 5%. **Uses**: Mouthwash, stain remover, washing meat, cleaning countertops, appliances, plants, humidifiers, whitens laundry. Helps seeds sprout.

 Laundry Soap (homemade): In a stainless steel pot, combine 1 bar of Fels Naptha Laundry Soap, 1 cup (250 mL) washing soda and 1 cup (250 mL) Borax. Once the mixture has melted, pour into a 5-gallon (18 L) pail and fill with hot water; stir. Cool, then use.

- **Lemon Juice**: Stain remover, mild bleach, especially effective when combined with cream of tartar. To brighten socks, boil them in lemon juice and water for 20 minutes.

- **Meat Tenderizer (Unseasoned)**: Protein stain remover, wash in cold water.

- **Pine Sol**: Removes black grease from flooring.

- **Rhubarb Leaves**: Boil in water to clean burnt pots.

Rhubarb

Rubbing Alcohol: Great for grass and ink stains. Remove stains on counter-tops, e.g., Kool-Aid, tea, tomato-based sauce, etc. To clean granite countertops, combine 1 tbsp. (15 mL) rubbing alcohol, 1 tbsp. (150 mL) dish soap in a spray bottle; add enough water to fill. Spray and wipe off.

Scouring Powder: Mix 2 parts baking soda with 2 parts washing soda. Wear gloves.

- **Shaving Cream**: Basically whipped soap with glycerin. **Uses**: Great spot remover on carpet, clothing and upholstery (use sparingly, a little squirt goes a long way). Scrub with a toothbrush and rinse. Use shaving cream to keep squirrels and cats out of car engines. Removes ink and dirt; cleans upholstery, cleans grease from hands, rinse with water. Prevent mirrors and goggles from fog-ging up by applying shaving cream and then wiping off. Removes ball point pen ink on upholstery and some leathers.

- **Toothpaste (Non-Gel)**: Cleans crayon off walls, removes rust in bathtub. Eliminates small scratches on glass. Removes fish smell from fingers.

- **Washing Soda (Sodium Carbonate** – cousin to baking soda). **Uses**: Cleans toilets, sinks, ovens (rinse with vinegar), range hoods, exhaust fans, stainless steel pots, stainless steel pans, garden tools, barbecue grills, utensils, outdoor fur-niture. Cleans silver, copper, gold, concrete floors, whitens laundry.
  Note: Contains no bleaches or phosphates but is caustic, wear gloves. Removes blue and green mineral deposits on stainless steel (Soak in washing soda and water for 10-20 minutes. Rinse).

- **Water**: Less than 1% of all the water on earth is available or clean enough to drink (the rest is salty or frozen). Water is by far the number one household superstar. Before scrubbing with soaps and detergents try plain water.

Wax Polish Recipe for Bare Wood: Melt ½ lb. (500 g) beeswax. Remove from heat, add 1 cup (250 mL) mineral spirits (white spirit/paint thinner). Polish.

Solutions 2

Introducing Household Superstar ... Olive Oil!

Olive oil is a symbol of knowledge, abundance, peace, health, power and beauty. It has been revered for thousands of years, and with good reason.

- Olive oil is one of the most beneficial dietary fats. It is a monounsaturated "heart healthy" fat and can actually help reduce cholesterol levels in your body.

- When selecting a good-quality olive oil be suspicious of low prices. You are not likely to find true extra-virgin oil for less than $12.00 for 16 oz. (500 mL). Look for imported oil certified by IOOC, DUP, DO, COOC or HEPO. Be wary of any imported oils not marked with these logos. Salads and dips (for the best flavor and health benefits) make sure oils are less than 1 year old. You can use older oils for cooking as the heat somewhat affects the health benefits anyway. Choose oils stored in dark-colored or opaque containers. Light damages oils, so store in a dark place.

- The use of various types of olive oil varies according to personal taste. Light olive oil should be chosen when you want a very subtle flavor. Light refers to color and flavor, not fat. Extra-virgin (cold-pressed, first pressing) oil enriches the flavor of meat, fish and vegetables, and is best for salad dressings and tossed pasta.

- Olive oil is not a good choice for deep-frying because it has a low smoking point; super canola is a better choice if you're planning to deep-fry. Light olive oil is best for baking and cooking, however, olive oil will not produce flaky pastry.

- **Polish diamonds** by wiping the stone with olive oil on a soft cloth.

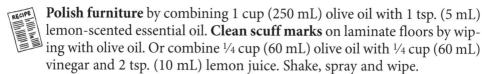

Polish furniture by combining 1 cup (250 mL) olive oil with 1 tsp. (5 mL) lemon-scented essential oil. **Clean scuff marks** on laminate floors by wiping with olive oil. Or combine ¼ cup (60 mL) olive oil with ¼ cup (60 mL) vinegar and 2 tsp. (10 mL) lemon juice. Shake, spray and wipe.

- **Shine shoes and soften leather** with olive oil before wearing them. Before commercial products hit the market, olive oil was consistently used on leather. To gradually soften leather, apply the oil with a soft cloth, wiping off the excess, every day for a week.

- Pour a few drops of olive oil onto a soft cloth to clean stainless steel appliances. Wipe the stainless steel to remove excess oil. Olive oil is not greasy and is effective at removing fingerprints.

- Unstick a zipper by using a cotton swab to rub a small amount of olive oil over the teeth.

- To cure a squeaky hinge, cut a circle the size of a washer out of felt and soak it with oil. Remove the hinge pin, put the washer on it and reinsert.

 For a delicious **Greek Salad**: Combine ½ cup (125 mL) extra-virgin olive oil with 2 tbsp. (30 mL) red wine vinegar, add salt and pepper to taste. Pour over a mixture of chopped tomatoes, unpeeled cucumbers, green peppers, red onion, dried oregano and black olives. Top with feta cheese. Enjoy!

COSMETIC USES FOR OLIVE OIL

- Add 3 tbsp. (45 mL) olive oil to bath water to soften dry skin.

- Remove makeup by applying olive oil to skin and wiping with a soft cloth.

 Make your own **Night Cream**: Combine ½ cup (125 mL) olive oil, 2 tbsp. (30 mL) vinegar and ¼ cup (60 mL) water. The oil softens and moisturizes skin while the vinegar lightens discolorations, kills bacteria and loosens dead skin. Dampen your face before use.

- Before hopping into bed, apply a small amount of olive oil to feet to soften heels and toes.

- Reduce static in hair by combing through with a small amount of olive oil. Olive oil also makes a wonderful hair conditioner.

Spread the Word about Peanut Butter

Peanut butter went public in 1904, patented by Dr. Kellogg who developed it as a meat alternative. Peanut butter is healthy and, even more importantly, it was "The King's" favorite food (yes, of course, I mean Elvis).

 Mice love peanut butter even more than cheese. Following is an aggressive approach to **capturing mice using peanut butter**: Put 2 tbsp. (30 mL) antifreeze into a 5-gallon (18 L) bucket with a lid. Cover the bucket and cut a 4" (10 cm) hole in the lid. Make a ramp so that the mice can climb up and fall in. Spread peanut butter around the hole. If you do not want to harm the mice, leave the bucket empty and, after they fall in, take them at least (1.24 miles) 2 km from your home/camper before releasing them. You can also spread peanut butter on glue boards or mousetraps (kill or non-kill). **Tip:** One common solution to keeping mice away when camping is to spread the contents of a box of fabric softener sheets around the camper or tent (even on the outside). Some people swear by this while others recommend peppermint oil on Irish Spring soap slivers.

- When you are camping and run out of shaving cream, use peanut butter as a substitute.

- Use peanut butter to remove gum from hair. The greasy consistency causes the gum to slide out.

- Fill holes and cracks in walls with smooth peanut butter; cover with paint.

Best Peanut Butter Cookies: Combine ½ cup (125 mL) butter or margarine, ½ cup (125 mL) white sugar, ½ cup (125 mL) brown sugar, 1 cup (250 mL) smooth or crunchy peanut butter, 1 egg, 1½ cups (375 mL) flour, ½ tsp. (2 mL) baking soda, ¼ tsp. (1 mL) vanilla and ¼ tsp. (1 mL) salt. Drop onto baking sheet. Bake at 350°F (180°C) for 8 minutes, or until lightly browned.

- Natural peanut butter is made without additives and needs to be refrigerated.

- When shopping for peanut butter, look for peanut butter made with dry-roasted peanuts. Peanuts contain more than enough fat, therefore this is a healthier choice than peanut butter made with peanuts "roasted in oil."

- Great news – peanut butter is high in vitamins A and E, folic acid, calcium, magnesium, zinc, iron, fiber, thiamin, niacin, potassium, pantothenic acid and phosphorus.

- Even better news – there is no cholesterol in peanut butter. Cholesterol is found only in products from animal sources (meat and dairy). The peanut is not a nut, but a legume related to beans and lentils. Like olive oil, peanut butter is primarily mono-saturated fat, which isn't linked to heart disease. However, beware of the fat. Peanut butter is high in calories and too much of any fat can increase the risk of heart disease.

- Have you ever wondered why peanuts are considered a meat alternative? Both contain protein, but unlike meat, nuts also supply fiber.
  Warning: Never eat moldy peanut butter; it could be contaminated with a fungus called, aspergillus.

- The difference between "natural" and "commercial" peanut butter is that some manufacturers may add hydrogenated oil, sugar, salt and some preservatives.

- Add 1 tbsp. (15 mL) peanut butter to burnt gravy.

 Natural Peanut Butter Recipe: Pour 1 tbsp. (15 mL) peanut oil into a food processor, gradually add 3 cups (750 mL) unsalted, dry roasted peanuts; blend to desired consistency. Increase the recipe as needed.

DID YOU KNOW?

- Arachibutyrophobia is the fear of getting peanut butter stuck to the roof of your mouth.
- Women and children typically prefer smooth peanut butter while men prefer chunky.

November is Peanut Butter Lovers month.

Solutions 2

The Buzz About Household Superstar ... Honey

- Honey is considered the only food that includes all the substances necessary to sustain life. History has recorded honey as the most used medicine in ancient Egypt. During World War I, honey was mixed with cod liver oil to treat soldiers' wounds.

- Typically 25-50% sweeter than sugar. It consists of equal parts sucrose and fructose and is one of the least refined sweeteners available. Dark honey has a stronger flavor than light honey. When baking, it is not necessary to use the highest quality of honey since it will be heated during cooking. Substitute 1 cup (250 mL) white granulated sugar for ¾ cup (175 mL) honey (reduce liquid in recipe by ¼ cup/ 60 mL).

- Honey is a healthy choice! It contains vitamins and antioxidants similar to spinach, but is fat, cholesterol and sodium free.

- **Raw honey**: Honey that has not been pasteurized, clarified, or filtered – provided it is of the highest organic quality – is your best choice. Look for honey that states "100% pure."

- **Regular honey** is translucent; creamy honey is usually opaque and is made by adding finely crystallized honey back into liquid honey.

- Honey is one of the oldest foods in existence. It was found in the tomb of King Tut and was still edible. Honey never spoils; one reason for this is its high sugar content and acidic pH which help to inhibit microorganism growth.

- Keep honey in an airtight container so that it doesn't crystallize. If your honey has crystallized, place the container in hot water for 15 minutes, it will return it to its liquid state. Honey that is kept at colder temperatures tends to thicken, while honey that is kept at higher temperatures has a tendency to darken and have an altered flavor.

- Brush warmed honey over ham and bake for 1 hour and 15 minutes in a pre-heated oven (or longer if using a slow cooker). Baste ham every 10-15 minutes with honey glaze. During the last 4-5 minutes of baking, turn on broiler to caramelize the glaze. Remove from oven and let sit a few minutes before serving.

- Honey causes food to brown, therefore, when baking with honey, reduce cooking temperature about 25°F (-4°C).

- Soothe sore throats. Opera singers often consume 1 tsp. (5 mL) of honey before going on stage.

- Use honey to sweeten tea, or even coffee. Getting used to the flavor may take time but after awhile coffee with sugar tastes strange.

- When making cookies, replace the sugar with honey. The honey keeps the cookies softer in texture. Be sure to deduct 3 tbsp. (45 mL) of liquid from the recipe.

 Honey Bath: Put ¼ cup (60 mL) warm honey in a glass with 5 drops of lavender oil. Add 1-2 tbsp. (15-30 mL) of the honey-lavender mixture to your bathwater. Relax and enjoy.

- Honey is great as a facemask because it has the ability to attract water. Warm honey and apply it to skin. Honey has a high content of alpha hydroxyl acid and is safe for sensitive skin.

- Use honey as a hair moisturizer. Mix honey with olive oil and condition hair. Be sure to wash your hair thoroughly before going outside.

 Honey Butter: Blend ½ cup (125 mL) butter with ½ cup (125 mL) honey. Beat thoroughly and store in fridge.

Kitchen Secret: Out of honey? Substitute 1¼ cups (300 mL) sugar dissolved in 1 cup (250 mL) water.

HONEY TRIVIA #1:

How many flowers must bees tap to make 1 lb. (500 g) of honey?

HONEY TRIVIA #2:

How far does a hive of bees fly to bring you 1 lb. (500 g) of honey?

#2: Over 55,000 miles.

#1: Two Million flowers.

ANSWERS:

- **WARNING: DO NOT FEED HONEY TO BABIES!** Their immune systems are not yet developed enough to resist the bacteria.

Get Creative with Household Superstar ... Vinegar

Vinegar is created from grains, fruits, honey, potatoes and whey as bacteria converts alcohol into acetic acid. Numerous studies show that common household vinegar kills 99% bacteria and 82% mold, while many common products claiming to be disinfectants have proven to be ineffective at cleaning.

- **To kill weeds**, spray on vinegar at full strength until the plants die.

- There are few **odors** worse than that of vomit in an automobile. Remove the lingering odor by placing a bowl of white vinegar on the floor of the car.

- Clean **dirt and stains** on car flooring with a mixture of 1 part water and 1 part vinegar.

- Say so long to stray cats lurking around a child's **outdoor sandbox**. Pour vinegar along the outside edge of the box, this will keep the cats from using it as a litter box.

- Pour 1 tbsp. (15 mL) vinegar into a drywall or plaster mix to keep it from drying too fast.

- **Water lines in a vase** can be washed away by placing a towel soaked with vinegar inside the vase. Make sure that the paper towel touches every edge. Let sit for a few hours and clean.

Germ Buster: In a spray bottle, combine 1 part water to 1 part vinegar and a few drops of lavender essential oil or tea tree oil. Use this solution to **kill germs** on bathroom fixtures, clean off soap scum, wipe away mildew and grime from bathtub tiles and shower curtains.

- **Reduce fading** on jeans and velvet corduroy by adding 1 cup (250 mL) vinegar to the wash. **Tip**: Wash jeans inside out, they will last longer. Also, vinegar added to the final rinse helps reduce lint and static on clothing.

- To take the **crease out** of dresses, skirts and pants after letting down a hem, spray the fabric with vinegar before ironing.

- To **slow down mold growth** on cheese, dampen a paper towel with vinegar and wrap it over the cheese.

- If you use bleach to clean your toilet bowl, do not mix bleach with vinegar, toilet-bowl cleaner or ammonia. The combination of bleach with any of these substances produces a dangerous gas.

 To **clean copper and brass**, combine ½ cup (125 mL) vinegar with 1 tbsp. (15 mL) salt.

Make your own **anti-fog spray**, mix ¼ cup (60 mL) white vinegar with 4 cups (1 L) tap water.

- **Clean your washing machine** by rinsing hoses and unclogging soap scum. Pour 1 cup (250 mL) vinegar into an empty washing machine and run a regular cycle.

- Vinegar is an excellent remedy for **soothing sunburns**. Apply vinegar to the sunburnt area, shower and repeat twice (your skin will thank you).

- **Dry, itchy skin** is a sure sign that winter is on the way. Beat the itch by adding 3 tbsp. (45 mL) vinegar to bath water.

- Say good-bye to smudges on eyewear. Wipe each lens with a drop of vinegar and rub with a soft cloth.

- Help **poached eggs** retain their shape by dropping 1 tsp. (5 mL) vinegar into the pan of water.

 Tenderize meat while killing bacteria by marinating the meat in vinegar. Soak the meat in ¼ cup (60 mL) vinegar for a 2-3 lb. (1-1.75 kg) roast. Marinate overnight, then cook; do not drain or rinse the meat. Add herbs to the vinegar when marinating if desired.

 Recipe for French Vinegar Dressing: In a bottle, combine 1 tsp. (5 mL) salt, ½ tsp. (2 mL) sugar, ¼ tsp. (1 mL) pepper, 1 clove minced garlic, ½ tsp. (2 mL) paprika, ⅓ cup (75 mL) vinegar and ⅔ cup (150 mL) vegetable oil. Cover bottle, shake and refrigerate for up to a week.

- Enjoy a variety of flavorful vinegars on salads and in marinades. Try apple cider, malt, wine, balsamic and the increasingly popular fruit and herb vinegars.

QUESTION:

I dyed my hair last night and accidentally got some of the dye on the white closet door (it's regular paint on the wood door). I tried to take it off, but it was already set in. Any idea how to get rid of the stain without actually repainting the door? Thanks, Stéphanie

ANSWER:

Use a combination of 50/50 baking powder and vinegar. Rub the area with an S.O.S pad, the stain may remain at first but don't give up, continue applying the solution and scrubbing the area until it disappears.

Solutions 2

Secrets from a Household Superstar ... Cabbage

Cabbage has a long history, since at least 400 BC. Cultivated in the West, it was looked upon as a valuable medicine.

To get rid of **cabbageworms**: Add 1 cup (250 mL) salt to 1 gallon (4 L) water; spray onto plants. Two applications are needed and the cabbage will remain unharmed. **Tip:** When setting out cabbage plants it is best to pull off the largest leaves so that only the center remains, they will grow more successfully.

- Sprinkle baking soda in your garden to keep rabbits from eating the cabbage. The baking soda will not hurt the animals.

- To clean carpet spots – slice a raw cabbage in half, brush the carpet with the cut side of the cabbage.

- A great way to polish pewter is to wipe the metal with a cabbage leaf and then buff with a cloth.

- Improve oily skin by drinking a daily cupful of cabbage cooking liquid.

- The Canadian Cancer Society recommends eating cabbage on a regular basis. Its high carotene content lessens the risk of cancer and other diseases.

- When making cabbage rolls, put cabbage heads in a freezer for about 2 days. Remove from freezer, place in a colander and defrost overnight. Core the cabbage and the leaves will be limp and perfect for rolling.

- Wash stale cabbage in salt water and a few ice cubes. The cabbage will regain its freshness and any germs will be destroyed.

- To add a different flavor to sandwiches, add shredded cabbage as a substitute for lettuce.

- After steaming cabbage, toss with melted butter, toasted nuts, minced onions. Yum!

- Say good-bye to cabbage odor during cooking by adding baking soda, vinegar or lemon juice to the water, or place the end slice of a loaf of bread on top of the cabbage or drop a walnut, a piece of bread or a chili pepper into the pot. **Tip:** Lemon juice in the pot also helps prevents water from changing color.

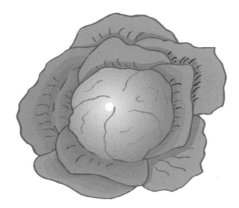

- Store cabbage uncut to prevent vitamin C loss. Place the uncut head in a perforated plastic bag and store for up to 2 weeks in the refrigerator crisper. If cabbage is cut, wrap the remainder in plastic, refrigerate and use within a couple of days.

- Cabbage is a very versatile vegetable that can be prepared many different ways: cooked or raw it is perfect for dishes ranging from corned beef, cabbage soups and stews, stir-fries, and cold salads such as coleslaw. Or allow it to ferment to produce sauerkraut. Cabbage can also be used as a wrap around fillings.

- Not only are there several ways to prepare cabbage, this vegetable is available in a variety of different forms, take your pick: Green Cabbage, Red Cabbage, Savoy, Brussels Sprouts, Napa, and Bok Choy.

 Recipe for **Oodly Noodly Cabbage Salad**. Combine 4 cups (1 L) shredded cabbage or bok choy, ¼ cup (60 mL) chopped onions, 1 pkg. flavored instant dry noodles, ½ cup (125 mL) toasted slivered almonds and ½ cup (125 mL) shredded carrots. **Dressing**: seasoning pkg. from noodles, ½ tsp. (2 mL) salt, 2 tbsp. (30 mL) sugar, ½ tsp. (2 mL) pepper, 3 tbsp. (45 mL) sesame seed oil (or more if desired) and 3 tbsp. (45 mL) vinegar. Pour dressing over salad and mix well. This recipe is great for sharing at potlucks! *Submitted by Darrin and Edith Muzyka.*

It's Soooooo Healthy!

Mark your calendars – February 17 is World Cabbage Day.

Cure More than a Headache with a Household Superstar ... Aspirin

Aspirin was 100 years old in 1997, and Americans consume 42 tons of it per day. Aspirin is a trade name for acetylsalicylic acid, a common pain reliever, but what else is it good for?

- Consider sharing some Aspirin with your **garden plants**. Tests last year at the Organic Vegetable Garden at the University of Rhode Island in Kingston showed that spraying a water solution containing Aspirin increased the yields and quality of tomatoes, eggplant, basil and other vegetables.

- If your **car battery** is dead and there is no one to jump start it, try this amazing trick. Drop 2 Aspirin tablets into the battery, the acid in Aspirin gives the battery acid one last charge.

- According to some experts, the acid in Aspirin helps to kill bacteria in the water, thereby prolonging the life of cut flowers.

- In a large bowl, dissolve 1 crushed Aspirin in a gallon (4 L) of water. Place this solution in a spray bottle and spray on your house plants. Most plants actually produce salicyclic acid. This is also the active ingredient in Aspirin. By spraying your plants you are helping boost their immunity.

- Drugs can save our lives, but they can also be dangerous if we use them in the wrong way. This is why medicines have labels that tell us how to use them safely. It's important to know how to **read the labels** on medicine bottles, like Aspirin, so that safe dosages are taken. Also, sometimes 2 medicines are perfectly safe when taken separately, but they can become toxic if taken at the same time!

- Most people realize that **giving Aspirin to children can be dangerous**, but they don't know why. Aspirin has been linked to **Reye's syndrome**, a rare but deadly illness that can affect the liver and brain.

- Aspirin can eliminate the problem of **dandruff**? Just crush and powder 2 Aspirin tablets and add to your shampoo. Leave the mixture on your scalp for 2 minutes. Wash and rinse well to completely remove the Aspirin particles.

- Swimming in a chlorinated pool can affect the color of light-colored hair. Return hair to a more natural shade by dissolving 6-8 Aspirins in a glass of warm water. Rub the solution into the hair and let it sit for 10-15 minutes. Rinse well.

 To relieve the itch of **bug bites**, dissolve 4 Aspirins in ¼ cup (60 mL) of rubbing alcohol. Rub it on the bites, either with a cotton ball or your fingertip. The Aspirin works for the pain and the alcohol disinfects the area.

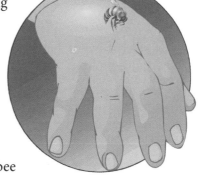

- To relieve the pain of **bee stings**, dissolve 1 Aspirin with just enough water to make a paste and apply it to the bee sting to remove the pain.
  Tip: "Preparation H" also works on bee stings.

 Soften hard calluses on your feet by grinding 5-6 Aspirins into a powder. Make a paste by adding 1 tsp. (5 mL) EACH lemon juice and water. Apply the mixture to the affected areas, then wrap your feet in a warm towel and cover them with a plastic bag. Stay off your feet for at least 10 minutes, then remove the bag and towel and file down the softened callus with a pumice stone.

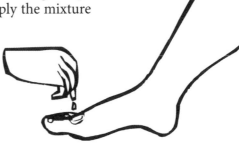

 To remove warts, dissolve 1 Aspirin in just enough water to make a paste. Cover the wart with the paste and a bandage. Leave for several days.

- **For canker sores**, wet an Aspirin and put it on the canker sore. This may sting for a moment but it is an effective way to get rid of canker sores.
  Tip: An even faster way of taking the sting out of cankers sores is to rub an unlit wooden match on the area, then put yogurt on the canker sore until the yogurt dissolves.

Household Superstar ... Cola Can

Many of us love to drink it, but where else does cola shine?

- To zap the rust from your hitch ball, fill a deflated balloon with cola. Fasten the balloon over the ball and let sit for a day. Remove the balloon and scrub the hitch ball with an S.O.S pad.

- Rub cola on mosquito and bee stings to take away the itch.

- Clean corrosion off batteries by pouring cola onto car battery connections to remove buildup.

- When the cat and the dog have a fight, leaving a trail of blood on the driveway. Pour cola onto the area, it eats the blood off the concrete and rinses clean with water, unlike sawdust and kitty litter. Cola also takes grease off driveways. Saturate concrete overnight; rinse the next day.

- Don't throw out flat cola; scrub the toilet with it to remove rust and grime. **Tip:** Pour a can of cola down a sluggish drain to unclog.

- Keep rats and mice away by setting out a bowl of cola, they can't handle the carbonation.

- To clean a hamster cage, empty the cage and pour cola over the bottom. Wait 5 minutes and scrape with a putty knife; it cleans like a dream.

- Clean your kettle by pouring in a 12½ oz. (355 mL) can of cola and letting it sit for 8 hours. Rinse and wipe.

 To **tenderize ham,** place a ham in a pan and pour a 12½ oz. (355 mL) can of cola over it; cover with aluminum foil and marinate for 3 hours before baking. Bake as usual. Save the drippings for flavorful gravy.

 Marinate steak in cola to tenderize it, or pour 2 x 12½ oz. (355 mL) cans of cola into a slow cooker with chicken or beef for a delicious flavor. **Tip:** Add a can of cola to your next pot roast to tenderize it.

- To soothe minor stomach aches, drink a few sips of flat cola.

- Antique photos by soaking them in flat cola. Using a baking pan, pour enough cola on a photo to cover it. Wait about 40 seconds and carefully wipe the picture. Dry it with a blow dryer. Test this on an undesirable image before trying it on a precious one.

- Remove gum from your hair by soaking the area with cola. Leave for 5 minutes and wipe off.

Use Household Superstar ... WD-40

WD-40 came out of a research project for a rust-preventative solvent and degreaser for missile parts. Only 4 people know the recipe and they claim that nothing in the solution can hurt you.

- Clean and lubricate lawn mower blades with WD-40.
- Spray WD-40 between cinder blocks to prevent weeds from growing.
- Lubricate bike gears by applying WD-40.
- Spray WD-40 on umbrellas to help them open and close.
- Spray a dry paint stain with WD-40. Let sit for 20 minutes and wipe.
- WD-40 removes stickers, duct tape, decals and price tags.
- WD-40 lubricates squeaky hinges, sticky doors, can openers, folding chairs and prevents wicker and rocking chairs from squeaking.
- Use WD-40 to remove crayon from: the dashboard, furniture, screen doors, toys, chalkboards, plastic, shoes, carpet, wallpaper and walls.
- Oven windows are hard to clean. Spray WD-40 on a cloth and wipe the window; scrub with an S.O.S pad. Rinse well with vinegar and water.
- A spritz of WD-40 will take care of glue on carpet as well as grime in the grout of ceramic bathroom floors.
- Loosen rusty nuts and screws with WD-40.
- WD-40 cleans coffee stains and ink from leather.
- Spray showerheads and bathroom fixtures with WD-40 to prevent rust.
- WD-40 is effective for cleaning water spots on shower doors.
- Most importantly, remember that WD-40, works wonders as a lubricant, adhesive, rust and ink remover. My brass cymbals had thirty-year-old stuck-on duct tape, the best solution I found for removing the adhesive was WD-40 in combination with an S.O.S pad. The cymbals also shone!
- To clean the bottom of an unplugged iron, spray WD-40 onto a cloth, wipe. Rinse well.

Household Stress? Call S.O.S!

In 1917 a salesman named Edwin Cox invented aluminum cookware. As he attempted to sell the pots and pans, he found that buyers complained about the difficulty of cleaning the aluminum. He then decided to utilize the abrasive nature of steel wool and dip it repeatedly into soapy water. The steel-wool pads were so popular that they exceeded the sale of the pots. Edwin opened a factory manufacturing small round scrub pads and he called them S.O.S pads, which stands for "Save Our Saucepans."

- Store S.O.S pads in the fridge or freezer or a sealed plastic bag to prevent them from developing rust.

- Store any kind of steel wool away from flames or heat sources; it is very flammable.

 For a wonderful **Multi-Purpose Cleaner**: Combine 1 tsp. (5 mL) borax, ½ tsp. (2 mL) washing soda, 2 tbsp. (30 mL) vinegar, ½ tsp. (2 mL) liquid Castile soap (made with olive oil and soda). Add 2 cups (500 mL) very hot water. Pour into a spray bottle and shake well. Spray on appliances, floors and house exteriors; scrub with S.O.S pads.

- Use S.O.S pads and water to remove nail polish from carpet (some elbow grease required). Nail polish can also be wiped away by using shaving cream or rubbing alcohol. Test on a small area first.

- Clean a vegetable peeler blade with S.O.S pads. The peeler will work better and sharpen itself at the same time.

- Clean burnt-on food from pots and pans by using baking soda and a little water. Bring the solution to a boil and then scrub with S.O.S pads.

- A dampened S.O.S pad will take off even the nastiest new or old scuff marks with very little elbow grease.

- Clean a dirty iron bottom with a dampened S.O.S pad. Then warm the iron and run it over a piece of waxed paper to restore the shiny finish.

- Scouring with an S.O.S pad and a few spoonfuls of ketchup can clean copper-bottomed pans.

- Avoid using S.O.S pads on cast-iron pots and pans. Instead, heat a thin layer of oil in the dirty pan; just before the oil begins to bubble, let it cool down. Then wipe the pan clean.

- Remove burnt-on hair spray from a curling iron by spraying the metal rod with WD-40 and scrubbing with an S.O.S pad.

- To maintain a shiny oven with little effort, wipe the interior with washing soda dissolved in a little water and an S.O.S pad. Rinse with vinegar and water. Take the racks out of the oven and soak them overnight in a bathtub filled with hot water and 1 cup (250 mL) of washing soda. In the morning the grime on the racks will slide off easily.

- Steel wool is graded from extra-coarse to super-fine. Coarse grades are used for removing heavy grime or smoothing or cleaning surfaces in disrepair. Finer steel wools are ideal for cleaning chromed steel, ceramic tiles, polished stone, plain porcelain, stainless steel and removing wax on floors.

To get rid of **Watermarks on Wood**: Use super-fine steel wool and apply with a solution of ½ cup (125 mL) vinegar combined with ½ cup (125 mL) water, let sit 20 minutes. Gently scrub the area. Next, using a soft cloth, smooth on a coat of furniture wax (e.g., Bri-Wax). **Caution**: When dealing with older furniture so the finish is not damaged.

WHY IS IT THAT S.O.S PADS HAVE NO PERIOD AFTER THE LAST "S"?

S.O.S. is the universal distress signal and cannot be trademarked. Leaving off the last period allowed Edwin Cox to register his product with the Patent Office.

Solutions 2

Don't Throw Out Your Newspapers!

After you have read your newspaper:

- Stuff crumpled-up newspaper inside suitcases to take away any musty odor.

- Roll newspaper and stuff into leather shoes to preserve the shape and keep them smelling fresh.

- In a winter emergency, stuff newspaper under your shirt if you are cold. You will be surprised at what a great insulator it is!

- If you have a fridge with a bad odor and have cleaned it thoroughly with baking soda and water, try newspaper. Unplug the fridge and remove the drawers. Stuff crumpled-up newspaper into the fridge; pack it tight and leave it for 3 days. The smell will disappear! *Submitted by Glenda Armstrong.*

- Wash and dry windows with newspaper to avoid streaks and save money on paper towels. Make sure that the paper is at least 3 days old so that the ink doesn't leave a mark.

- Use newspaper (at least 3 days old) as padding underneath a tablecloth, this makes spills easy to wipe up and protects the wood.

- Newspaper is handy and large enough for making sewing patterns.

- Clean your barbecue grill with newspaper. When the grill is warm (not hot), place damp sheets of newspaper on the grill. Close the lid and leave for 20-30 minutes. Wipe the grill and smile.

- Lay newspaper on the bottom of a garbage can to reduce odors.

- Place several layers of newspaper underneath rugs to help keep the house feeling warmer in the winter and cooler in the summer. The newspaper layer also makes the rug feel more cushioned.

- **Make your own fire starter**: Loosely roll together several layers of newspaper and tape the outside layer closed. No added chemicals are necessary. Leave for at least a few days (the longer the better) so that the paper dries out and burns better. Position the roll inside a fireplace or bonfire pit. Light and enjoy, it lasts longer then you might think! *Submitted by Sharon Nerbas.*

 To prevent newsprint from fading, dissolve ½ cup (125 mL) Milk of Magnesia in 1 quart (1 L) club soda. Soak paper for 1 hour. Lay flat to dry.

Solutions for Spiders!

While you should want a healthy spider population outside, it is reasonable to assume any spiders inside your house will be unwanted guests.

- Spiders are good guys! Sometimes they end up in the wrong place however; keep in mind that they are amazing predators of pest insects. Spiders consume far more insects than do birds. Worldwide, spiders eat enough insects in 1 year to equal the weight of the entire human population.

- The best way to keep the indoor spider population down is to have a clean house. Spiders may enter through cracks and openings. Seal buildings with caulk, screening and weather stripping to keep them from entering.

- If you have too many spiders, put hummingbird feeders outside. Hummingbirds eat huge numbers of spiders. Cats are another deterrent.

- Commercial chemical sprays only destroy spiders if the spray lands directly on them. The spray does not have a long-lasting residual effect. A spider can walk over a sprayed surface within hours and not be affected.

- Tape or seal storage boxes, especially in basements and garages.

- Regular vacuuming or sweeping of windows, corners, storage areas, basements and other seldom-used areas help deter spiders and their webs.

- Put insect glue boards in areas where spiders might be found, e.g., behind toilets, under sinks, behind refrigerator, washers, water heaters, attics. These boards are available at hardware stores.

- Outdoor lighting attracts insects, which in turn attract spiders. Regularly sweep, mop, hose or vacuum spiders off buildings and away from windows and doors.

- For homes with an uncontrollable infestation of spiders, consult a professional. Sorptive dust (containing diatomaceous earth or amorphous silica gel) is applied to cracks and crevices in attics, walls, voids and other enclosed areas. This is a last resort.

- **Spider Bites:** Relieve local swelling and pain by applying an ice pack, ammonia or alcohol directly to the bite area. In case of a severe reaction, consult a doctor immediately and, if possible, take along the spider for possible identification. Specific antivenom is available to treat some widow spider bites.

- Clean cobwebs from high ceilings by dragging a helium ballon (attached to a string) along the upper edges of the walls. Static electricity attracts the cobwebs to the balloon; pull the string and wipe off the balloon.

Ways to Make Wasps Buzz Off!

Give us a break! Dry summers reduce the mosquito population but bring about a new challenge.

- If wasps are not bothering you, leave them alone. Knocking down a wasp nest is a risky business; surviving wasps will be angry and may attack. Also, they often rebuild nests in a new, nearby, location.

- Stay still. If wasps are nearby the best defense is to remain calm. Like other creatures (even humans) they will attack if they feel threatened, and when they do they often signal for backup.

- Wasps sleep at night, therefore any steps to destroy the unwelcome visitors should be taken at night. If you fill the exit hole in the nest with expandable foam, they will suffocate.

- Wasps love garbage and food. Put out a fast-food hamburger or an open can of tuna laced with boric acid (or powdered cleanser, e.g., Ajax). The wasps will gobble up the toxic food (do this for 2 or 3 days to get all of the wasps). Commercial wasp killer and poison are also available in stores. Wear protective clothing before you make your move. **Caution**: The contents of this food may be harmful to other creatures as well as humans.

- If wasps build a nest under your front steps or deck each year, beat them to the punch. Blow up a brown paper lunch bag and close it with a string. Tie the balloon bag underneath the porch and they will think there is already a nest in that area.

- To discourage wasps from invading your patio, tuck dryer softener sheets underneath the patio umbrella or string an inflated brown paper bag under the umbrella rim or on a nearby tree.

- Sitting outside will be more peaceful if you place an open bottle of beer away from the sitting area.

- Repel wasps from areas such as apartment balconies by setting out a dish of cloves and lemon slices.

- For trees or bushes with ripening fruit, distract wasps by hanging a half-full jam jar (with a small hole in the lid) on a tree branch. The wasps will be unable to exit the jar.

- In an emergency, rub a bee or wasp sting with dirt and a bit of water. While this will not take all of the discomfort away, it does relieve some of the pain. Cold compresses, calamine lotion and vinegar are also effective. A paste of meat tenderizer and water is another option. If an allergic reaction to the sting occurs, call for immediate medical attention.

- If a pet receives a bee or wasp sting, rub the area with a paste of baking soda and water. **Note:** Bees may leave a stinger behind, wasps will not, making them capable of repeated stings.

- Make your yard unattractive to wasps. Seal cracks; clean-up fallen fruit; keep compost away from the house. Seal garbage; keep soil damp and grass short.

- Put away your yellow summer clothes or give them to someone you don't like. Wasps are attracted to the color yellow! In fact you can go one step further and place painted yellow bricks at a distance from your house to encourage wasps to leave you alone.

- Wasps don't like garlic.

 For a Wasp Deterrent: In a spray bottle, combine 1 tsp. (5 mL) dish detergent and 1-2 cups (250-500 mL) water; drop in 2-3 whole garlic cloves. Leave overnight. Spray clothes and skin with the repellent mixture to deter wasps as well as mosquitoes.

- While some people use gasoline, fire or smoke to get rid of wasps, this is very dangerous, especially during a dry summer season.

Big Ideas to Get Rid of Small Annoying Flies

 Set out a container filled with ¼ cup (60 mL) vinegar and 1 drop of liquid soap. Place it in an area away from any open fruit.

- Set a trap by filling a jar with overripe fruit. Insert a paper or metal funnel into the mouth of the jar. Flies can get inside but not out.

- If left alone fruit flies can multiply at an incredible rate and lay up to 500 eggs a week. When searching for breeding sources, the obvious place to check is fruits and vegetables that are stored in open areas. Also, recycling bins and hidden areas, e.g., behind the fridge and stove.

- If you do set fruit out, place basil in fruit bowls to deter the little bugs. You can also plant pots of basil outside near entrances or windows.

- Fill a vinegar bottle with wine or apple cider vinegar or beer mixed with clamato juice to drown flies. The flies will enter the hole but are unable to exit and drown. You can also purchase attractive wasp and fly catchers.

- Beer and soda attract flies; rinse cans and drop into a sealed garbage, or set the containers on the counter as bait.

- Eliminate moisture around the sink because it attracts flies. Wipe down all kitchen surfaces with pure vinegar.

- Fruit flies can lay eggs inside drains. Pour a half-gallon of undiluted bleach down the drain and leave it overnight to kill eggs. Do this with the windows open or when the house can be temporarily vacated.

 Recipe for **Fly Eliminator**: In a saucepan, combine 2 cups (500 mL) milk, ½ cup (125 mL) sugar and ¼ cup (60 mL) ground pepper; simmer for 8-10 minutes. Pour into shallow dishes. Flies will attack the solution and suffocate.

- Fruit flies can hatch in plant soil. Check the soil when you water. Put yellow sticky flytraps into the plant pots.

- Do not over-water your houseplants. Let the soil dry before rewatering. The flies will not produce eggs in dry soil.

 Get rid of spiders, houseflies and fruit flies by combining 10 drops Lemongrass Essential Oil with ¼ cup (60 mL) of water. Pour into a spray bottle and apply to plants, counters, sidewalks, doors and windows.

- **Flea Flee:** Zap fleas on your dog by bathing it in salt water. Once the dog is dry, rub its fur with baker's yeast.

Discourage Uninvited Guests

Some people love them while others hate them. Whether dealing with cats, rabbits, squirrels, bats, mice or ants, it's time to take back your yard! Keep in mind that animals are diverse, what works for one may not necessarily work for another.

MOTHBALL WARNING: Although mothballs may be effective in discouraging critters, it is IMPORTANT to note the health warnings linked to mothballs. Mothballs/flakes contain either naphthalene or paradichlorobenzene. Naphthalene is 3 times as poisonous as paradichlorobenzene and **may cause serious blood problems in children and animals**.

- A great way to keep any animals from bothering your plants is to offer them an edible alternative:
  - **Rabbits** love dandelion plants, leave a few dandelion plants somewhere, like behind the shed (you can deadhead the flowers to keep them from self-seeding) and the rabbits will find them.
  - **Deer** love birdseed (it is grain), so, if you don't want deer eating your shrubs, try putting out a pan of birdseed in some unobtrusive place (maybe in the dandelion patch).
  - **Squirrels** love birdseed but they love sunflower seeds and peanuts more, put a pan of sunflower seeds underneath your bird feeder. Peanuts are slightly more expensive; sunflower seeds are cheaper; buy in bulk.

- To prevent small animals from getting into the birdbath, place a shallow pan of water out of sight, e.g., under a bush (remember to put some rocks into it so that any mice that fall in can get back out), and change the water every couple of days to keep mosquitoes from breeding in it.

- Make a **Scarecrow** by nailing 2 sticks together to form a cross. Loosely staple old clothing to the wood so it can flap in the breeze. Pinwheels also work.

- **Cats in the garden**: To make your yard unattractive to cats, plant a patch of catnip away from your yard. Add mulch to garden areas, e.g., pinecones, or large flat river rock. Position rose bush branches along the ground where cats like to step. If you do not have rose bushes ask your local garden center, they may be willing to donate thorny branches. Alternatively, lay down mats that have upward facing points (cats don't like to step on prickles). Or plant "rue." Its lovely blue foliage that makes the garden attractive, but cats detest the smell. Keep cats out of the garden by sprinkling coffee grounds or onions on the soil.

- Spray an intruding cat with a hose and give it a firm "no" when it comes toward the yard; better yet, install an activated motion sensor sprinkler system. Whenever the cat comes by, "bam," he gets water in the face. Some cats love water, so for those we need to move on.

- Pet and garden stores sell products, e.g., predator urine and cat repellents or you can make your own. **Cat Repellent**: Combine and sprinkle: 2 parts cayenne pepper, 3 parts dry mustard and 5 parts flour, the drawback is that you will need to reapply the mixture after rain. Or spray plants with a pepper and water solution or pour bleach around the edge of the garden. **Tip**: Use the same spray to keep cats away from indoor houseplants as well as the Christmas tree.

- **Ants**: There are many solutions for getting rid of ants, e.g., a line of chalk on the floor, laying fabric softener sheets on the ground, sprinkling pepper, cinnamon, mint-flavored tea bags or coffee grounds in drawers. My favorite "Ant Away" solution is a mixture of: 1 cup (250 mL) borax and 2 tbsp. (30 mL) icing sugar. Place the mixture in a container in areas away from pets, kids and hungry neighbors. Or place the mixture in a shaker and sprinkle over cracks. **Note**: Although these are extremely effective solutions, if an outbreak has gotten out of control, purchase a product specifically designed to kill ants fast, e.g., Raid for Ants with a 2-week residual kill.

- **Squirrels**: Keep squirrels off birdfeeders by sprinkling them with pepper. To make **Squirrel Repellent**: in a spray bottle, combine 2 tbsp. (30 mL) Murphy's Oil Soap, 2 tbsp. (30 mL) hot sauce and ¼ tsp. (1 mL) cayenne pepper.

- **Mice**: Shaving cream is the answer for these cheese-loving creatures. Soak cotton balls with shaving cream and position them where mice have a tendency to scurry, e.g., attics, cupboards and car engines.

- **Potato Bugs**: Here is a tip from a 100-year-old man who has gardened most of his life. To kill potato bugs, boil rhubarb leaves in water. Pour the cooled solution over potato plants.

- **Rabbits**: Surround the garden with milk jugs lined with sand. The idea is that the rabbits will chew on the milk jugs instead of the plants. Human hair (from the local salon) sprinkled in the garden dissuades both deer and rabbits. As well, planting marigolds in and around the garden repels rabbits. Mothballs also tend to work, as does a combination of Tabasco sauce and water sprayed onto plants.

- **Deer**: They are beautiful to look at but have a tendency to feast on gardens. **Deer Repellent**: In a spray bottle combine: 2 eggs, 2 cups (500 mL) water, 4 garlic cloves and 2 tsp. (10 mL) Tabasco sauce. Reapply after rain.

- **Bats**: Although some people encourage bats as a way of reducing population of the much-loved mosquito, others find them creepy. Bats love dark areas such as tree houses and sheds. Keep doors closed when not in use and, if the area will not be occupied for long periods of time, place mothballs in corners.

- **Snakes**: Unfortunately, there is no snake repellent or trap that will keep snakes from a house or yard. Any substance that would deter a snake would probably make the house uninhabitable for humans. Preventive measures include eliminating breeding areas for snakes by removing wood and trash piles and sealing up or screening openings where snakes can enter the house. Mothballs, sulfur and a product called Snake-A-Way are worth a try. If you are desperate, construct a fence using heavy galvanized screening 3' (1 m) wide with ¼" (6 mm) mesh. Bury the bottom of the fence 6" (15 cm) below the soil surface.

- **Skunks**: At this time, there are no chemicals registered to control skunks. Mothballs may be an effective deterrent for the smelly critters but they will not succeed if the skunk has already marked its territory. Screening off the area with 2" (5 cm) wire is the best solution for skunks.

Skunk Spray Recovery Solution: Combine 4 cups (1 L) hydrogen peroxide, ¼ cup (60 mL) baking soda and 1 tsp. (5 mL) liquid dish detergent; mix, lather and rinse. **Keep away from eyes.**

- **Flies**: It would be too obvious to mention that keeping windows and doors closed is the key to a lower fly population in the house. Flies lay eggs in garbage, therefore it is important to cover garbage and discard frequently. An open beer can or bottle situated near a fence will lure flies away from guests.

Fly Deterrent Recipe: In a bowl, combine 3 cups (750 mL) water, ¼ cup (60 mL) sugar, ¼ cup (60 mL) vinegar and 3 tbsp. (45 mL) dish soap. Leave bowl where flies tend to congregate. **Tip:** Placing bowls of dried lavender in the room will also deter flies.

- **Cereal Bugs**: Prevent bugs in food by storing dry foods in plastic containers with tight-fitting lids. Also, place a bay leaf in packages with grains or, even better, freeze flour instead of keeping it in the cupboard. Lay bay leaves in kitchen drawers and sugar sacks to keep crawling insects away.

- **Mothballs**: Instead of sprinkling mothballs along the ground and allowing the chemicals to seep into the soil, consider the following device as a great way to reap the advantages of mothballs while keeping them separate from the soil. Fill an empty shampoo bottle with mothballs; replace the lid on the bottle; poke holes into the bottle so that the smell of the mothballs is noticeable. Lastly, pierce the bottom of the bottle with a stick and push the stick into the ground so the bottle is elevated.

Household Solutions

Ways to Reap What You Sow

- When purchasing fruiting plants, select dark green plants that do not already bear fruit. Studies have shown that the presence of fruit will stunt the plant growth when it is replanted and the total yield may be reduced.

- **Tomatoes**: With tomatoes, a gardener's biggest headache is often cut-worms. To prevent an infestation, place a 3-4" (8-10 cm) nail or toothpick in the ground next to each stem as plants are planted or wrap strips of newspaper around the bottom of stems. Alternatively, surround stems with a paper cup (cut out the bottom). Add 1 tsp. (5 mL) of milk powder to the soil when planting tomatoes to help the ripening process.
  Tip: Tomatoes can be grown in a pot or a bucket. Remember to stake plants. *Submitted by Arnie Stahl.*

- **Carrots**: It is important to thin carrots as they begin to grow. Pull out seedlings so that 2" (5 cm) spaces remain to allow them room to grow. Like tomatoes, carrots can be grown in containers at least 12" (30 cm) deep. Over-watering lightens the color of carrots. But, when harvesting, drenching the carrots first makes them easier to pull.

- **Lettuce**: One of the easiest vegetables to grow, lettuce is affected by few pests and is perfect for the gardener who lacks a green thumb. Lettuce may be planted in a garden, pot or hanging basket. Line a pot with a garbage bag and add soil. Sprinkle with seeds (very important). Harvest when the growth is 3" (8 cm) but leave 1" (2.5 cm) intact to encourage new growth. One lettuce basket can supply 3 harvests (keep moist). **Trivia**: Did you know that lettuce is a member of the sunflower family?

- **Beans**: Beans are healthy and delicious, and enrich the soil. Beans respond well to straw mulch.

- **Onions**: The onion family is huge, ranging from garlic through to leeks, chives and shallots. Grass clippings between rows of onions make a great weed killer. Shallots are a smart garden choice. They are easy to grow and their subtle flavors are highly valued by chefs. Plant shallots 6-8" (15-20 cm) apart with the roots facing downward (so that the tips are just barely below the soil). Shallots may be planted in a container. **Tip**: Use a cut onion to polish gold.

- **Garlic**: Hold off on planting garlic until the fall. Hot weather forces garlic to go to seed, waiting until the fall will give you a better crop.

- **Corn**: If you have a small garden but want the delicious flavor of freshly harvested corn, opt to plant several small rows side by side rather than a long single row. **Bird Tips**: Protect corn from birds by covering the plants with netting. To keep birds and small animals away, secure thin, dark-colored string in a zigzag pattern across the bed about 1¼" (3 cm) above the ground level. Also, keep birds away from the garden by placing a pinwheel nearby. Or attach aluminum foil strips to a stake. An artificial owl placed high in the garden is also a deterrent.

- **Peppers**: Warm weather and sunny days make hot peppers hotter and sweet peppers even richer. For extra flavor, plant peppers where they will get plenty of sun. Peppers should sit even with the soil, too shallow result in dried-out stems; too deep gives them stem rot. Add newspapers around plants and a layer of straw or grass.

- **Asparagus**: The benefit to planting asparagus is that it is a perennial. The disadvantage is that you will not be able to harvest it for about 5 years. Plant asparagus in full sun and rich soil. When asparagus begins to grow, cover the greens with soil and fertilize 3 times a year.

- **Cucumbers**: As cucumber plants grow, pinch off the growth tip after 6 or 7 true leaves have developed to encourage side shoots.

- **Potatoes**: Forget all the cultivation, digging trenches, etc. Cut potatoes into pieces with 3 eyes (sprouts) on each piece – allow cut edges to dry for a day. Spread black plastic over the soil and secure it. Make slits and put the cut potatoes through the plastic with a trowel. No weeding required. Or grow potatoes in a big pot, be sure to fertilize and choose a pot with drainage holes.

- **Peas**: The biggest problem with peas is root rot; it causes foliage to turn brown and die. Ensuring soil is well-drained and rotating the crop each year will help. **Note**: Be careful not to over fertilize, too much nitrogen can create large pods housing small peas.

- **Strawberries**: Easy to grow, delicious and as an excellent ground cover, strawberries require no staking and are very popular for planting in children's gardens. Strawberry plants grow well in pots, planters and hanging planters. Most strawberry plants provide 3 years of fruit bearing.

Garden Tip: Don't give up on broken plant stems, instead splint the broken area with a drinking straw slit lengthwise.

Solutions 2

The Grass is Always Greener on the Healthy Side

- Lawns usually suffer from over watering rather than under watering. Don't keep soil soaked or the roots will suffer. Water in the early morning, just before sunrise. Don't water again until you can see footprints after walking across the lawn. **Tip:** Lawns need about 1" (2.5 cm) of water per week. Turn sprinklers on once or twice a week, not every day.

- When repairing lawn patches with grass seed, apply the seed thickly, until it starts to overlap. Create 1 layer with no spaces between.

- If you decide to fertilize your lawn, use a slow-release product in the spring. The fertilizer will provide nutrients throughout the season.

- Be wary of low-cost grass seed mixtures. Improved seed varieties generally cost more but each healthy seed can improve lawn quality.

- Use a weed-controlling fertilizer once or twice a year to reduce the amount of weeds, you will also provide nutrients to the soil.

- When applying lawn fertilizer, be careful not to fill the applicator with the spreader parked on the lawn. Doing so can result in grass burn.

 Eye-Poppin-Green-Grass Recipe: For 1,000 square feet (93 square meters). To thicken up your lawn, mix together 3.8 cubic feet (0.107 cubic meters) peat moss, 2 cubic feet (0.056 cubic meters) vermiculite, 2 large bags compost, ½ lb. (250 g) nitrogen lawn fertilizer and 2 lbs. (1 kg) grass seed. Spread over the lawn and keep moist for 2 days.

 For really **Green Grass,** spray cola onto your lawn once a month. To get dual benefits from cola, combine and spray: 12½ oz. (355 mL) can of cola, 1 cup (250 mL) ammonia and ¼ cup (60 mL) liquid dish detergent (green grass and no bugs). Or combine 2 tbsp. (30 mL) Epsom salts and 1 gallon (1 L) water.

- Cut the lawn with a sharp blade. A dull blade tears at the grass, leaving a jagged brown line across the top of the cut grass. **Tip:** For average household usage, the blade should be sharpened once a month.

- Mow the lawn when the grass is dry and 3-3½" (8-9 cm) tall. Never cut shorter than 2-2½" (5-6 cm). Following this guideline will keep natural nutrients working in the lawn (this rule is more flexible when using mulch mowers).

- If grass is long and needs to be raked, compost it. Allow it to break down into a brown powder, then apply it to the lawn as you would fertilizer.

- Using mulch mowers not only cuts down on yard maintenance, it also makes grass greener. Hauling away grass clippings can actually take away your lawn's natural fertilizer.

- Each year approximately 75,000 people are injured by lawn mowers. Very few accidents occur because of mechanical failure. Be safe and know your lawn mower (read the manual). Dress appropriately (never mow with sandals or bare feet and always wear long pants). Clear the area before mowing. Beware of the blade, never attempt to unclog a jammed lawn mower while the engine is running, disconnect spark plugs to ensure the mower cannot start. When mowing on a hill, travel across the slope.

- Things to think about before purchasing a lawn mower:
  - Decide on the right-sized machine for the job (6.5-6.75 hp is a good size for the average yard).
  - Do you want a mulcher/leaf collector?
  - Look at the deck. A mower with a deck made of ABS plastic will not rust and is more resistant to scratches.
  - Does the handle fold? This will make it easier to transport and store.
  - If gas powered, find out what kind of fuel is best.
  - Ask about the warranty.
  - Front wheels that are castered (swivel), make it easy to change direction. Large back wheels make it more maneuverable.
  - Deciding between self-propelled vs. push mower? Most self-propelled mowers have an option to switch to a push mower.
  - Does the mower come with a bagger?
  - Does the machine have a manual choke and throttle?
  - Does the brand have a good reputation? Read consumer reports.

 Grass Stain Remover: Rub clothing with blackboard chalk, toothpaste or molasses (leave overnight). Or combine 1 tsp. (5 mL) ammonia and 1 tsp. (5 mL) hydrogen peroxide or denatured alcohol (test for color fastness before applying products to stain).

- To deter grasshoppers, plant basil around flower bed borders. Grasshoppers will eat the basil and leave the plants alone.

Happy Cutting!

Solutions 2

Cheers for Raking Leaves

- Why rake leaves? A thick layer of leaves sitting under the snow will literally suffocate grass. To make leaves compost faster they need to be shredded before adding them to the compost bin.

- The best combination of leaves for compost is 25 parts brown to 1 part green. This mixture should create a good balance of nitrogen and carbon.

- After raking the yard, do not throw away the leaves. Spread them over the garden and wet down. Work them into the soil in the spring; as the leaves decompose they add nutrients to the soil. Leaves are loaded with minerals. Too much carbon will cause the pile to break down slowly. Add to compost: grass clippings, coffee grounds, crushed eggshells, fruit and vegetable peelings. Do not add meat or dairy foods.

- The words "mulch" and "compost" are not the same. Compost must be decomposed completely because its function is to release nutrients into the soil immediately. On the other hand, mulch should not completely decompose. It is a weed suppressor. Mulch should be kept in a separate bin from compost and can be used immediately.

- An easier way to get leaves and debris into garbage bags is to make a funnel. Use an old laundry basket that fits inside the garbage bag, cut out the bottom of the laundry basket to make the funnel.

- If you use blisters as a reason not to rake, you may not want your spouse to see this tip. Slip a piece of foam-pipe insulation around the rake handle and you can get back to work.

- Wear maxi pads on knees to prevent sore knees when gardening.

- When raking leaves and pine needles be sure to also remove "thatch." Thatch is the layer of dead turf-grass tissue between green vegetation and soil. Rake deeply to remove thatch.

- A power rake is another option to raking. It is similar in size to a lawn mower and is designed with a series of vertical blades that work hard to rip away thatch.

Household Solutions 2 with Kitchen Secrets

- Once you've gotten the leaves together, consider raking them onto a vegetable bed. Sprinkle lime or ashes over top. Also, include a layer of dirt between each layer of leaves and moisten with water. Turn the pile once a month until snow arrives.

- When caring for your rake, clean all metal surfaces with a wire brush. Coat the metal with vegetable or motor oil to prevent rust.

- **Garden or bow rake vs. bamboo rakes**. A garden rake is metal and stronger than a bamboo rake. It falls apart less frequently but tends to rip into the lawn. A bamboo or lawn rake is lighter and often less expensive. **Tip**: Keep your eyes open for ergo rakes, they have a contoured handle and pressure is exerted on the rake instead of on your body.

- Prevent wooden handles from drying out by boiling a rag in oil. Rub the oil-soaked rag along the handle to prevent cracks in the wood.

- Resist the temptation to repair a broken handle. The result will be weak and you can injure your hands. However, instead of throwing out a good rake purchase a new replacement handle. You may need to file it to make it fit. Bring the rake to the store to test the size.

- Avoid climbing ladders to inspect for leaves and debris. Tape a handheld mirror to the end of a broom and check out the dirt from below.

- Bury a handful of nails around trees with yellow leaves; water regularly. The tree can extract the iron it needs from the nails, causing the leaves to green up.

- Line a pot with a diaper before adding the soil and plant; you will need to water less as the diaper keeps the moisture in.

- Clean houseplants by wiping the leaves with the soft inside of a banana skin. The banana skin brings up a lovely shine and removes dust while adding a good smell. Don't have a banana? Use a little milk on a soft cloth to wipe down the leaves of houseplants to keep them shiny.

 House and Garden Bite-Back Recipe: In a 1 gallon (4 L) milk jug, combine 2 tbsp. (30 mL) dish detergent, 1 tbsp. (15 mL) rubbing alcohol, dash of Tabasco sauce, 1 tbsp. (15 mL) canola oil and enough water to fill the jug. Pour mixture into a spray bottle and apply as needed. *Submitted by Jan Cooper.*

Curb Appeal Sells!

You only get 1 chance to make a first impression, 49% of all houses sell because of curb appeal. Also, keep your house looking great for yourself.

- Asking your real estate agent for advice (before putting your home on the market). If the house needs a new coat of paint, choose the colors together. The realtor will have a good idea of the best colors.

- Look at the house from a buyer's point of view. Take a photograph of the exterior (front and back) to judge the house objectively. Make a checklist of everything that needs to be done before the "for sale" sign goes up.

- Clean up that junk! A potential buyer does not want to see children's toys, wheelbarrows, pet dishes, tools, garbage cans or lawn mowers lying around the yard. The cleaner the yard, the faster the house will sell. I once bought a house because the S.O.S pads were carefully put into their own little container underneath the sink. If people pay attention to the little details it sends a message that they probably pay attention to the big ones.

- Get rid of whimsical statues, windmills and nameplates. Potential owners want to picture themselves living in the house. The personal stuff must go! **Tip**: Move cars off the driveway.

- Spruce up the mailbox. Although it may seem like an insignificant detail, it's a small effort that can make a big difference. Purchase a new mailbox or paint the old one. Make sure it is clean and attractive.

- Lighting is always key. Exterior lights should be clean, working and rust free. Light the walkway with tasteful solar powered lighting.

- Plant containers add charm and personality to a garden. Clay pots may be a little more money but also show that you take great care of your yard. Use the pots to draw the buyer's eye away from unappealing areas, e.g., fire hydrant or a place where grass did not grow. **Tip**: Window boxes are also a nice addition depending on the style of the home.

- Wash windows. People often say that if the windows are clean, the rest of the house will likely be well maintained. It's all about first impressions. **Tip**: Clean with water or water and vinegar, wipe the windows and dry with newspaper that is 3 days old or older. Wash windows in the morning or on cloudy days.

- A narrow walk leading to the front door is uninviting, a walk that curves is much more appealing. Consider building a walkway that is wider where it meets the public walk and wider as it reaches the front steps. Two people should be able to walk together side by side.

- Use brick, stone or concrete pavers to give the illusion of a wide walkway. Dig out the grass on either side of the walkway and lay a line of the chosen paving materials along both sides. Fill in with natural-colored mulch.

- Around trees scatter mulch not more than 2-3" (5-8 cm) deep. Do not pile the mulch up on the tree trunks. Cut the grass, clear the weeds; trim the hedges, shrubs, trees and plants.

- Although you consider your pets adorable, take them away while potential buyers stop in. Ask yourself, if you did not have pets of your own, would you rather sleep in a hotel that allows pets or not? Your yard will be viewed as much cleaner if no pets are around.

- Invest in a good-quality door and door handle. The front door says a lot about your house, as well as giving the buyer an added sense of security. You can faux finish a door, giving it an antiqued look, depending on the style of your house. The front door may have a bold paint color to create a focal point. Getting advice before painting can help you make a great choice. **Tip**: The front steps should be clean, replace old carpets or paint the stairs to freshen them up.

A fresh coat of paint is worth the effort because potential owners will see the exterior as they drive up. However, before rushing to paint, try washing the exterior. **To wash wood or aluminum siding**, use a solution of 1 cup (250 mL) detergent, 1 quart (1 L) chlorine bleach and 3 gallons (11 L) of water. To clean vinyl siding, hose it down and wash with a mild detergent. Rinse with the hose.

- Porches and decks make a wonderful addition to many homes. Check for spider webs, peeling paint, dirty furniture, dead plants and a dirty barbecue. Clean is key! I once bought a car because the owner's garden was well maintained. In my mind if he was a perfectionist in the yard he would likely have taken great care of his vehicle (but enough about me).

- When selling your house, remove all hanging towels in the kitchen. Nobody wants to see damp used towels, washcloths, hosiery or robes in the kitchen, bedroom or bathroom. The same rule should be applied whenever company is coming over.

Keeping Your Deck Looking Dreamy

- Decks are a popular way to add living space to a house. Due to the harshness of nature, maintenance is an essential part of owning a deck.

- Call your local hydro or power company before you dig to check the location of underground wires, pipes, gasoline and electrical lines in your yard. This is a free service.

- In general, when a deck is stained the protection will last 2 years. However, if the deck is exposed to excessive sun or mildew, it will need to be protected every year.

- Contrary to popular belief, stain your deck within a month of installation to protect against the elements, preventing premature warping and cracking of deck boards.

- Three characteristics to look for when choosing a finish:
  - A good sealant will contain ultraviolet protection to reduce the damaging effects of the sun.
  - The finish should be waterproof, not just "water resistant."
  - If mildew is a potential problem, the finish should contain a mildewcide (found in most wood preservatives).

- If you love the natural look of wood and want to apply a clear waterproofing agent only, think twice. With no pigment in the stain, you will not get maximum protection because stain deflects the sun's rays. **Rule of thumb**: The more pigment in the stain, the more protection the deck will get. PVC (polyvinyl chloride) is a great low-maintenance decking material. The drawback is that if the product is not properly installed the expansion and contraction of the plastic due to hot and cold temperatures may result in shifting over time.

- Choosing not to maintain your deck does not mean it will fall down immediately. However, dirt, mold and algae can build up on untreated deck surfaces, making them unsafe. Cleaning and sealing a deck will remove organic buildup and prevent splintering.

- Be cautious if cleaning with a pressure washer. It can inadvertently damage the deck. There are many commercial deck cleaners on the market. Read and follow all instructions. **Note**: Generally, the stronger the cleaner, the less scrubbing needed.

To clean away mildew, use a garden sprayer and the following recipe: Combine 3 quarts (3 L) water, 1 quart (1 L) bleach and 1 cup (250 mL) ammonia-free liquid dishwasher detergent. Apply; leave for 10 minutes; rinse. For tougher mildew stains apply the solution with a soft brush.

- **For grease stains,** use TSP (trisodium phosphate), washing soda or a commercial deck cleaner (powdered is normally more effective than liquid), e.g., M-83. If the wood has been treated you may attempt to remove the stain. If the wood is unsealed it will absorb the grease.

 Alternatively, **treat the grease stain** using the following technique: On a hot sunny day, make a thick paste of baking soda and rubbing alcohol. Apply this to the grease stain and cover with a black piece of sheet metal. Leave in the direct sun for 90 minutes. Lift the metal and remove the dried paste; wash with vinegar and water. Rewash with detergent and water; rinse. If the treatment did not work, sand the area and restain. **Tip:** To remove paint stains, apply lacquer thinner. Do not use this product on synthetic building materials.

- Candle wax on a sealed wooden deck can be removed using a putty knife and grease remover (test remover). Steam the wood clean by heating with a steam iron or apply hot water and a little pressure.

- When building a deck use screws instead of nails, they hold better.

- If woodpeckers have taken a liking to your deck, plastic owls or rubber snakes on the deck should keep them away.

- Setting planters and pots directly on the deck surface may cause staining. Place pots on a 2" (5 cm) square cedar board to create a space between the deck and planter.

- Faded canvas patio umbrellas can be rejuvenated with 2 coats of latex exterior paint. Latex paint has a certain amount of elasticity and can expand with the fabric.

Solutions 2

Concrete Ideas

- **To repair cracks in the driveway**: Begin by cleaning the area. Patch with crack-filler (a caulk-like compound), available at home-improvement stores. After applying the compound, smooth the area using a putty knife. For extra traction on the driveway, spread sand onto the wet sealer before it dries.

- For larger areas use cold-patch compound. Follow product directions, more than one layer may be needed. Flatten the patch by laying a piece of plywood over the repair and drive over it several times.

- Look at the difference between asphalt and concrete. Asphalt is flexible and may require several layers of application. Asphalt does not spread as easily as concrete and is generally weaker. Concrete is available in a wide variety of colors and textures. Concrete lasts 10 to 15 years longer than asphalt and is a rigid product. Compare prices before selecting.

- Concrete is no longer limited to the garage floor. Consider choosing cement countertops for the bathroom or kitchen. Cement countertops are made of sand, aggregate and water. Add colored glass pieces, mosaics or fossils to customize a design for your home (color choices are endless). **Tip**: Choosing cement for the backsplash instead of the entire countertop is also an option.

- Disadvantages to cement countertops include: hard-to-clean surfaces, the material is porous and therefore improper sealing can lead to stains; may crack; cutting directly on the cement will cause marks on the surface.

 To fight mildew stains on cement: Combine ½ cup (125 mL) of bleach with 1 gallon (4 L) of water. Use a spray bottle to apply, then scrub.

- **Zap grease stains on concrete floors**: Start with a stiff brush; sprinkle the wet concrete with dishwasher detergent. Let stand for 5 minutes and pour boiling water over the area. Scrub and rinse.

- **Muriatic acid** (hydrochloric acid) is also a concrete floor cleaner, although extreme caution must be used with this product. Apply the acid to the floor and scrub (follow instructions on bottle). Remember, muriatic acid can be added to water but **water cannot be added to muriatic acid**.

- **Cat litter** is another grease-stain fighter for concrete. Work cat litter onto the area until the stain fades. Sweep the area and spray on oven cleaner. Leave for 10 minutes, rub with a stiff brush and rinse using a pressure washer. **Tip**: Alternatively, use wood shavings in place of kitty litter, to soak up grease stains.

- Give your concrete floor a lift with fresh paint. Sweep and vacuum, then wash the surface using muriatic acid. Follow the directions on the bottle. Choose a paint that is 2 parts epoxy and speak to your paint dealer about proper application. Seal the floor and add a protective gloss finish, e.g., liquid acrylic finish.

- Concrete floors and driveways can be sealed to prevent staining. Concrete is porous and, without sealing, it absorbs stains. Floors must be clean before sealing, follow the paint dealer's instructions before applying sealer. Keep in mind that the surface cannot be walked on for 2-3 days after application.

- To remove glue from concrete surfaces begin by heating the area with a hair dryer or heat gun. Next, apply a contact cement solvent, rinse with warm water.

- **Oil stains**: Clean concrete driveways by spraying oil stains with oven cleaner. Leave the cleaner for 5 minutes (leaving the cleaner on too long can damage the concrete). Wash with a brush. **Tip**: In the same way cola is also effective for cleaning driveways, see page 18.

- To remove cement from fabric, scrape off residue, apply WD-40 to the stain, scrub and wash (do not toss the item into the dryer unless the stain is gone). If the stain remains purchase a cement solvent; read the label before applying the product to a textile.

 To clean stucco or brick: Combine 1 tbsp. (15 mL) dishwashing liquid, ½ cup (125 mL) washing soda, ½ cup (125 mL) hydrogen peroxide, ¼ cup (60 mL) borax and 1 gallon (4 L) of water. Spray the area to be cleaned with the solution and scrub. **Tip**: TSP and a pressure washer also work well to clean stucco or brick. **Tip**: To remove a white powdery buildup on brick or concrete, scrub with 1 part muriatic acid to 8 parts water. (**Use with caution**.) Rinse.

A Must-Do Annual Chores List

After the daily jobs are done ...

- **JANUARY**: Begin with the **Master bedroom**. Clean curtains, closets, drawers, dressers and bed linens; wipe down walls, baseboards and floors. **Tip**: To clean mini blinds, slip your hand into a sock and dip it into warm soapy water.

- **FEBRUARY**: Tackle all other bedrooms. Clean curtains, closets, drawers, dressers and bed linens; wipe down walls, baseboards and floors. If you really love clutter, set it free!

- **MARCH: Bathrooms**: wash curtains; clean out sink and tub drains, wash walls and floors; organize medicine cabinet (properly dispose of expired products); wash under the sink cabinets; clean out linen closets and turn old towels into cleaning cloths.

- **APRIL: Kitchen**: clean windows, walls, floors, sink, appliances; oil wood cabinets and furniture. Straighten items in cabinets and pantry; wipe the top of cupboards; replace old shelf paper. Save money by vacuuming the backs of appliances. **Spring clean the inside of your cupboards with the following solution**: Combine 1-2 cups (250-500 mL) vinegar, 1 cup (250 mL) ammonia (optional), ½ cup (125 mL) baking soda and 2 gallons (7.5 L) water. Cover hands with rubber gloves and use a small amount on a sponge to wipe each cupboard (from bottom up to prevent streaking). **Tip**: Before washing cupboards, vacuum the shelves.

- **MAY: Storage rooms**: clean out freezer, closets and bookcases, wash windows, shelves, walls and floors.

- **JUNE: Outdoor work**: clean awnings, sidewalks, outdoor furniture, garbage cans, windows and screens.

- **JULY: Living room**: clean curtains, walls, floors, furniture, coasters, picture frames, carpets and rugs. **Tip**: To clean pet hair off furniture, wear a damp rubber glove and run your hand along the sofa and chairs.

- **AUGUST**: Organize and clean out closets and dressers, hallway and stairs.

- **SEPTEMBER**: **Bathrooms**: clean walls, floors, drawers, cupboards, linen closet. **Tip**: If a bathroom rack is loose, remove the screws, wrap some cotton around them, dip into glue and replace screws (or nails) in original holes. Wait until glue dries before using the rack.

- **OCTOBER**: **Kitchen and dining room**: repeat the April tasks but include the china cabinet.

- **NOVEMBER**: **Family room**: clean toys and toss broken ones, wash windows, floors, walls and furniture. Polish silverware and inspect holiday placemats, dishes and decorations.

- **DECEMBER**: This is a busy time of year, so keep the jobs to a minimum. Take an hour to organize and clean the office and sewing room. If at all possible, try to tidy high-traffic areas (especially the bathroom). Be prepared to welcome drop-in company.

- **ADDITIONALLY, EVERY MONTH**: Vacuum air-supply and air-return registers; check that fire extinguishers are charged; clean garbage disposal by grinding up ice cubes (freshen with baking soda or a half lemon); check for cracks in caulking around sinks, bathtubs, toilets, countertops, backsplashes, faucets, windowsills; clean dirty filter in range-hood fan.

- **EVERY 6 MONTHS**: Check for exterior caulking cracks on windows; touch-up peeling paint; tighten screws and additional hardware; test smoke detectors and change batteries; lubricate doors, clean sliding door tracks with a silicone spray (not oil), oil moving parts of garage doors; check electrical cords for fraying parts; inspect roof, shingles, clean gutters and downspouts; have a professional checkup on air conditioner; inspect water lines and valves for leaks; check window and screen problems; clean exhaust fans in bathrooms and kitchen; weed out unused clothing that can be donated to appropriate agencies. Fertilize plants and clean them by hosing them in the shower; wipe ceiling fan blades; wash out the chest freezer using baking soda and water.

- **ONCE A YEAR**: Check attic vents for insulation blockage and signs of roof leaks; have chimney and furnace cleaned; remove water-heater residue according to manual; pressure-clean roof tiles, pool, deck, driveway and walks; clean dryer vent pipe (to prevent fire); shampoo carpets.

If It's Broken, Fix It!

- **Loose table leg**: Turn the table upside down and tighten all bolts. If the leg bolt continues to turn without getting tight, remove the bolt from the table frame. Wrap the bolt with Teflon tape (available in hardware stores). Reinsert the bolt and tighten.

- **Loose plastic laminate on countertop**: Clean under laminate with a cloth soaked with rubbing alcohol. While it dries, mix slow-curing epoxy and apply between laminate and countertop. Press and secure with heavy books. Leave for 2 hours. Scrape off excess epoxy with a sharp blade; let dry.

- **Dent in wood furniture**: Pour olive oil on a cloth and work into the table. Polish the entire table with a soft cloth. For larger dents, poke the dent with a pin in several places; lay a damp towel over the dent. Place a warm iron over it just long enough for the dent to swell back to size. **Note**: Take extra care when removing dents from varnished or antique furniture.

- **To fix a loose screw**: Dip it in glue or putty before you rescrew it. **Tip**: Provide extra grip to a screw by placing a wooden match in the hole. Or wrap strands of steel wool around the thread before replacing the screw.

- **Burn in carpet**: Cut away as many of the singed fibers as possible. Remove several strands of carpet from another area or extra carpet remnant. Glue carpet fibers into the burnt spot and press into place.

- **Squeaky floorboards**: Buy powdered graphite in a squeeze tube and force the powder between 2 floorboards (use a putty knife if necessary).

- **Moss build-up on roof or steps**: Sprinkle the area with powdered laundry detergent and wet down. Don't use in places that pets will lick.

- **Grease marks on wooden cupboard doors**: Clean cabinets with products that cut grease but do not create any additional build-up. Try mild liquid dish detergent and water or baking soda and water. Once a month or less, apply olive oil; every 6 months apply a thin coat of car wax. Let dry and buff.

- **Sandpaper wears out fast**: Fasten duct tape to the back of the sandpaper and each sheet will last up to 5 times longer!

- **Small hole or tear in mesh window screen**: Straighten any bent pieces of screen using a pointed tool. Dab the hole and surrounding area with a small amount of clear nail polish. Let dry; then reapply nail polish.

Hints to Make Bathroom Renovating Easy

- Decide before you start the project how much work you are willing to do. In other words, are you planning to tackle the walls, floor, paint the ceiling and baseboards? Knowing every task will help you determine the proper order for each project. **Take your blood pressure medication.**

- Make a list of necessary supplies before you start: paint (primer), rollers, tray, edger, painter's tape, ladder, tools, drop sheets, rags, head cover, etc.

- Place small objects in a plastic bag with the tool you used to take them out. This saves a lot of time at the end of the project.

- After removing the toilet, fill the sewer pipe with a garbage bag so that you do not lose any tools or valuables.

- Latex or oil? Apply nail polish remover to a cotton ball and rub it on the wall. If the paint comes off easily it is latex. **Tip**: Paint stores also carry test kits.

- Wash the walls with trisodium phosphate (TSP) or bleach and water in the case of mold damage.

- Paint the ceiling before you install the new flooring. **Tip**: Before pouring paint from a can, cover the rim with masking tape. After pouring, remove the tape, the rim will be clean and the cover will fit tightly.

- Use a primer before applying paint; primer will cover up wall imperfections and freshen the room by getting rid of odors such as pets and smoke.

- Cover your head when painting the ceiling, stretch-and-seal plastic wrap works well. Painting corners and borders first.

- Place a mat or drop sheet on and outside the work area to avoid tracking paint. **Tip**: If using old paint, strain it through pantihose to remove lumps.

- Install the ceiling light fixture after the paint has dried. **Tip**: Lighting is key for both mood and grooming. Overhead lights provide ambience, install a low wattage bulb or dimmer switch.

- After cleaning the latex paintbrush, dip it into a solution of diluted fabric softener or cream rinse to keep bristles soft.

- A large mirror will add depth to the room. Lights around the mirror provide task lighting. Sconce lighting is another option that emits a warm soothing glow while being bright enough for makeup application. *Special thanks to Margret Malaviya for these great tips.*

Ways To Keep From Flushing Money Down the Toilet

40% of all water used in a home is flushed down the toilet.

- When shopping for a new toilet, remember that there is little correlation between price and performance. Paying more for a toilet will not necessarily guarantee better flush performance.

- Before purchasing a new toilet, consider a dual flush system. This type of toilet saves an average of 26% more than single-flush 6-quart (6 L) units.

- Low-flush toilets use as little as 2 cups (500 mL) of water per flush. Regular flush toilets use anywhere from 6 quarts (6 L) to 13 quarts (13 L) per flush. Low-consumption toilets replace high-water-use toilets with 7 quart (7 L) per flush models. The disadvantage of low-flush toilets is that they may not be powerful enough to remove all of the waste every time. They also plug up easier than regular units.

- There are two basic types of flushing systems, pressure and gravity. With pressure-assisted flush, all waste is removed quickly, in 4 seconds. This system is slightly louder, allows no condensation or sweating on the outer tank and is typically more effective than gravity-fed. Gravity-fed flush uses the force of gravity and siphon "pull-through" action to empty the bowl. It has a smaller evacuation trap that forms a vacuum to pull water down.

- To check for a leaky flush valve, turn off the water and mark the water level with a permanent marker. Every once in a while check to make sure the water is hitting the mark, if not, you likely have a leak. Another way to check if you have a leak is to drop blue food coloring into the tank, if the water in the toilet becomes blue without being flushed, you have a leak.

- Before purchasing a toilet, measure the dimensions of the bathroom and the distance from the floor flange bolt holes to the rear wall. Older houses tend to have smaller bathrooms and are often sized for a 10" (25 cm) rough-in (new homes normally have a 12"/30 cm rough-in).

- To caulk or not to caulk? If this were a perfect world there would be no need to caulk around toilets. However, caulking is a good way to keep fluid from sneaking under the toilet where it can stagnate, reach the subfloor and cause problems.

- A flange is the bracket that porcelain toilets mount to. Over a period of time the metal ring can rust through. An alternate option is to choose stainless steel or brass flanges and screws. Make sure that the bolts you purchase are

long enough to penetrate the subfloor. **Tip**: If broken, new flanges can be purchased at all major hardware stores.

- Fixing a slow-flushing toilet may be a job best left to a professional. Anyone using muriatic acid to rectify a slow-flushing toilet should use extreme caution. Wear gloves and safety goggles, open all windows and turn on exhaust fan. Use muriatic acid according to package directions (**always pour acid into water; never add water to acid**).

- Clean a toilet by dropping 1 or 2 denture tablets into the bowl overnight. In the morning, brush as usual. **Tip**: To prevent bacteria build-up, flush 1 cup (250 mL) of baking soda down the toilet every week.

- When choosing a toilet seat look for style, color and shape. Modern toilet seats include a heat option that plugs in behind the toilet and can be turned off and on. Another new feature, toilet seats with nozzles that spray water, thereby cleaning with little effort.

- When water forms on the outside of a toilet tank it is likely due to condensation. To prevent condensation, insulate the inside of the tank or install an anti-sweat valve which will pipe just enough warm water into the toilet to prevent condensation. Or, shut off the water and drain. Apply a thick coat of car wax to the tank interior, then turn on the water.

- A recent study tested toilet paper brands for softness and dissolvability; Charmin Ultra was rated as the winner. However, in terms of the best buy, Scott won due to its strength, price and softness.

- Recycled toilet paper, tissues, napkins and paper towels may cost a little more but they also have benefits. Most recycled papers are not bleached with chlorine so they benefit the environment as well as your health.

- There are 2 basic plunger styles; flat or designed to fit. Flat is the best choice for the sink, bathtub and shower. However, a toilet requires a plunger with a flange designed to fit into the bottom hole. Plungers are available with high gloss or metallic handles. Plunger cases may be purchased and painted to match the bathroom or stamped with patterns or funny sayings. **Tip**: Toilet brush or plunger handles can double as reserve toilet paper holders.

WHO KNEW?

The first toilet stall in a public washroom is the least likely to be used. It is also the cleanest.

Step Onto the Best Flooring in Town

- **CERAMIC TILE: Advantages**: Very durable; water resistant; affordable; available in a tremendous array of colors, patterns and textures; easy to clean. **Tip**: Buy the best grade suited for your needs. Ceramic tile is rated from 1-5 with 1=least durable and 5=most durable. 1 and 2 are best for wall installation; 3, 4 and 5 are best for residential floors; 4 and 5 are great for commercial applications. **Disadvantages**: Cold to walk on (unless heated from underneath), matching replacement colors may not be available after 5 years because manufacturers constantly create and discontinue lines. **Tip**: Tile does not need to be sealed but seal grout to guard against discoloration in high-traffic areas.

- **CORK FLOORING: Advantages**: This product is more than 50% air which makes it lightweight; a natural sound absorber; resilient. It does not show dents or grooves, is allergy free and warm to walk on. Damaged tiles can be replaced. **Disadvantages**: Darker shades may fade over time; easily damaged by strong solvents; can stain and be permanently gouged. **Tip**: To clean cork flooring, use a few drops of dishwashing liquid (nothing gritty, as it can scratch the finish) or all-purpose cleaner and warm water. Sweep or vacuum frequently. Do not wet mop since water and other standing liquids will damage the floor.

- **HARDWOOD: Advantages**: Beautiful and warm to walk on; daily maintenance is non-intensive; available in a wide variety of colors and woods. **Tip**: Cleaning, do not use soap, wet-mop, oil-soap detergent or citrus products to clean. These choices may result in swelling, warping, joint separation and can void warranty. Purchase laminate or hardwood cleaners recommended by the manufacturer or products such as Torley's, Columbia or Cedar Squeaky. Whichever product you choose, it must say, "good for hardwood or laminate." Spray and mop or wipe. While Murphy's Oil may be fine for ledges and stairs it is not recommended for wood floors as it can strip them. For tough spots (oil, paint, markers, lipstick, ink, tar, cigarette marks) apply acetone and wipe (test on inconspicuous area first). **Disadvantages**: If not cared for properly hardwood can be damaged; it is not-scratch resistant and needs refinishing from time to time. However, hardwood is available with a ceramic finish, which is more scratch resistant than typical hardwoods because aluminum oxides are infused into the product. Remember: With hardwood you get what you pay for. To repair a hardwood floor, sand and recoat to open the surface pores. This allows you to reapply another coat of polyurethane and freshens the floor, making it look new again. **Tip:** Dark spots on wood floors are often caused by an exposure to alkaline substances which have been left to dry on the floor. Remove solvent-based wax with mineral spirits, this is flammable so be careful and ventilate. Apply vinegar to spots and leave for 3-4 minutes If stain remains try 4% oxalic acid but read the label carefully. If this does not work, call a professional.

 Homemade Hardwood Cleaner: In a bucket, combine ½ cup (125 mL) apple cider vinegar to 1 gallon (4 L) water. Dampen (don't soak the hardwood) a cloth and wipe on the floor and then rinse.

- **Heads Up!** Solid hardwood is made of solid wood. Engineered hardwood floors are made of cross-laminated layers of wood with a hardwood veneer top. The old name for engineered floors was laminate, but now the term "laminate" is used to describe synthetic hardwood floors.

- **LAMINATE FLOORING:** A manufactured process that sandwiches composite fiberboard material between 2 sheets of melamine, the upper layer may contain a sheet of real hardwood or may be a photo of wood with a thick sealant overtop. Before purchasing laminate, experiment with **The Hammer Test:** Bang the wood with a hammer, if it breaks or dents, choose a higher-quality product. It may cost more but the added investment will be worth it! **Advantages:** It is cheaper than most kinds of flooring; available in many different patterns and colors; can be installed by a relatively inexperienced handywoman (or man). Glued-together laminate is less popular than click-together laminate (click together is faster to install). Clean laminate with a dampened microfiber mop (add a small amount of olive oil if desired); once in awhile use manufacturer's cleaning product. Sweep or vacuum (do not use a beater bar). **Disadvantages:** Noisy; water spots are noticeable depending on the way the boards run; boards may pull apart or bubble; may heave if water is left on the surface. **Note:** Because laminate is intended as a floating floor, it may have a slight tapping sound as you walk on it. Certain manufacturers now offer an acoustical padding to muffle the sound. *Hammer Test contributed by Garry Nerbas.*

Household Solutions

- **LINOLEUM: Did you know that linoleum is not vinyl?** Linoleum, produced from linseed oil and flax in 1899, was popular until 1960 when vinyl made its debut. However, people tend to use both terms interchangeably. True linoleum is expensive and not readily available. **Advantages**: Environmentally friendly; wears better than vinyl because it is thicker; the color runs all the way through the material. **Disadvantages**: Needs regular waxing and polishing. Fairly maintenance intensive. **Tips**: Scuffed linoleum can be washed with an all-purpose cleaner. Apply 2 coats of water-based gloss urethane; allow 24 hours between each coat. Always use a liquid, non-abrasive cleaner. If linoleum is uneven in appearance it needs to be stripped, e.g., Magnum Plus UHS Stripper, and then covered with a thermoplastic acrylic floor finish, e.g., Succeed 90 by ZEP.

- **MARBLE FLOORING**: **Advantages**: Every piece is unique and beautiful, very durable. **Disadvantages**: High cost and maintenance.

- **PORCELAIN TILE:** Is made from a mixture of raw materials. Porcelain is completely non-absorbent and has outstanding mechanical characteristics, e.g., it can handle extreme temperatures very well. Today, porcelain tile comes in many sizes, colors and designs and is great for high traffic areas for the floor and wall. While cracked tiles are the risk during installation, as well as after installation, the chances are low if tile thickness is substantial.

- **SLATE TILE:** formed when ocean or riverbed sediments are compressed and heated by the earth's crust; components are quartz, chlorite, mica and calcite. **Advantages**: Hard wearing, natural stone; non-slippery because of its texture; comfortable to walk on; holds warmth in rather than reflecting it. Slate needs to be sealed with either water or solvent based acrylic sealer. Once sealed, it is protected from water, dust, grime and mud. **Disadvantages**: Expensive, but an investment, never needs replacing. Needs to be resealed about every three years.

- **VINYL FLOORING**: **Advantages**: Costs 70% less than most other flooring; easy installation; low maintenance; durable; available in many colors; moisture resistant, therefore ideal for kitchens and bathrooms. **Disadvantages**: Difficult to repair, tends to permanently discolor when a floor mat is left on it (due to the sulfur content in many floor mats). Another disadvantage is that glue may not hold, causing vinyl to bubble and corners to lift.

Caring for Granite, Ceramic and Marble

Although I do not claim to be an expert regarding marble, granite, terrazzo and slate, I have spent countless hours researching care procedures for these materials. Apply the following at your own risk and always test on an inconspicuous area.

- Before purchasing flooring, bathroom fixtures and countertops, etc., do your homework. There are far too many instances where people spend thousands of dollars on marble and granite only to be disappointed with the upkeep, staining and the care that they require. You can have a wonderful experience with these materials if you find out what the best choices are and where to get them. Talk to your neighbors, friends, co-workers, whoever has lived with the products that you are interested in. **Note:** High prices may not necessarily equal high-end products.

- To reapply a wax finish to unglazed **ceramic tile, quarry tile, slate and marble floors**, follow these steps: Begin by sweeping the area. Apply an instant wax stripper (dilute 1 part stripper to 3 parts water). Leave 3-5 minutes. Mop using a cotton-blend head. Rinse. Apply a neutral cleaner, e.g., hydrogen peroxide or ammonia. Dry and apply 2-3 coats of sealer. Finish with sponge mop. Dry.

- When washing any floor, wring out the mop until it is almost dry. Using too much water can dissolve protective coatings and loosen tile seams. Since it is difficult to get all of the cleaning solution out of the scrubbing mop, use a different mop to rinse.

- If you lay area rugs on stone flooring, prevent corners from curling by using peel-and-stick linoleum tiles, either cut into triangle shapes or leave as is. Fasten the sticky side to the curling carpet corners to keep them flat.

- Do not try to remove stains on marble or granite using orange juice, nail polish remover, shampoo, vinegar, wine or cola. Also, never use anything abrasive, stick with the cleaner suggested by the manufacturer. **Tip:** To remove candle wax from granite or marble, smooth on waterless hand cleanser.

- If small scratches occur on granite, apply a small amount of appliance or car wax. Do not attempt to fix larger scratches on your own, call a professional stone refinisher.

When dealing with water or oil stains on granite, use a technique called poultice. **To make a Poultice**: Cut 8 paper towels into pieces that are a little larger than the stain. Immerse them in acetone (from a hardware store – NOT nail polish remover) and place on stain. Cover the area with plastic wrap and tape the edges, using masking tape. Let sit for 24 hours. Let air-dry 4-5 hours. If unsuccessful, reapply until the stain is gone. **Tip**: Do not use a plastic spatula to apply the acetone because it will melt. Test on an inconspicuous area first.

- If the stain is coffee or wine, use strong hydrogen peroxide (30 or 40 volume) instead of acetone. Wear rubber gloves.

- **The lemon test**: People often wonder whether their countertop is sealed properly and whether it needs to be resealed. Pour a few drops of lemon juice onto the counter. If the juice sits on the counter the seal is good, if the lemon disappears into the counter you need to reseal. **Tip**: Use pH breathable sealers for marble and granite.

- To remove a dark ring in the granite around a bathroom faucet try "Lime Away."

- Before purchasing stone, slate, granite, etc., decide what you are looking for by asking yourself about: functionality, temperature exposure, color, texture, maintenance required, price and aesthetic appeal.

- **Consider every option and choose wisely**: tile, brick, stone, quarried slate (a fine-grained metamorphic rock that splits into thin smooth surface layers), limestone, Mexican tile, terrazzo (made by mixing different-colored marble chips with colored cement and epoxy), terra-cotta tile (slabs of clay fired for hardness), concrete, flagstone, granite or marble.

 To clean marble, terrazzo and slate: Make a paste using baking soda, water and lemon juice. Gently scrub the stain, rinse and dry. Windex may work but can strip the finish over time. **Tip**: Apply vegetable oil to sticky marble countertops.

- Like the look of **ceramic tile** but not the feel of walking on it? Consider installing ceramic tile underneath the dining room table only. Install enough tile behind the chairs so that they can be pushed out but still remain on the tile.

Piecing Together the Countertop Puzzle

With numerous countertop options available, it can be an overwhelming task to choose. Remember, you can make more than 1 selection, mixing and matching may be the answer to customize your kitchen needs.

- Before opening your wallet consider the following: durability, ease of cleaning, stain resistance, heat resistance, scratch resistance, price and your own personal design taste.

- In terms of cleaning, your best bet is to apply the product specifically formulated by the manufacturer (before experimenting with alternative solutions). Natural stones that are porous require a pH balanced cleaner, acidic or alkaline cleaners will abrade the surface. Avoid vinegar, lemon, lime or ammonia. Always rinse and dry.

- **SOAPSTONE**: A natural non-porous material, the main ingredient is talc. **Advantages**: Resists food stains, is not affected by household cleaners, acids, heat. Light sanding removes scratches. Does not need to be sealed. **Disadvantage**: Considered by some to be too soft for kitchen use. **Note**: Clean with soap and water. Can be darkened by applying mineral oil.

- **MARBLE**: This porous natural stone is beautiful and cool to touch. **Advantages**: Great for bathrooms. Consider adding a marble slab to the kitchen for those wishing to make candy or pastry. Costs less than granite. **Disadvantages**: Not as durable as granite. May require more sealing than granite (sealing will reduce staining). Seal 1-2 times per year. Susceptible to scratches and dulling. **Note**: Darker colors require more attention than light. Do not apply abrasive or acidic cleaners, wash with a damp cloth and dry. Refer serious scratches to a professional.

- **GRANITE**: A common coarse-grained, light-colored hard igneous rock (some say as old as the earth). **Advantages**: Does not scratch easily. Hard and durable. **Disadvantage**: Expensive and in most cases will have a seam. **Note**: Most granite requires sealing to prevent staining (check with manufacturer). Granite tiles are a less expensive choice than a granite slab. Do not use acidic products, e.g., lemon juice, vinegar or abrasive cleaners on surface. Wipe up spills immediately. **Clean granite stains** by making a paste using baking soda and water, or 3% hydrogen peroxide or borax and water. Using a soft cloth, wipe on then rinse. Don't use steel wool or abrasive sponges. For everyday cleaning, use the manufacturers' recommended cleaner or combine 1 tbsp. (15 mL) rubbing alcohol, 1 tbsp. (150 mL) dish soap in a spray bottle with enough water to fill the bottle. Spray on and wipe.

- **QUARTZ**: A natural incredibly smooth stone as tough as granite or marble but less porous and therefore less chance of staining. Quartz is made with 97% quartz and 3% color resin. **Advantages**: Does not need to be sealed or polished. Stain resistant. Cannot be scratched with anything other than a diamond. Wash with manufacturers' recommended cleaning products. **Disadvantage**: Price.

- **CORIAN**: An innovative product, Corian is an advanced blend of natural minerals and pure acrylic polymer. **Advantages**: Seamless sinks can be incorporated directly into an all-in-one counter. Does not need sealing. Approximately same price as granite. **Disadvantages**: Susceptible to stains and scratches. Cannot place hot items on counter. **Note**: Clean with soap and water, nothing abrasive. Sand out stains and scratches with a buffing kit, careful not to sand too often.

- **STAINLESS STEEL**: A generic name for a number of different steels. All stainless steels share a minimum percentage of 10.5 chromium. **Advantages**: Great for eliminating bacterial contamination. Heat and stain resistant and waterproof. Neutral color coordinates with any kitchen. Affects light and brightness of room. **Disadvantages**: Susceptible to fingerprints and scratches. **Note**: Cleans easily with a damp cloth, baking soda and vinegar or soap and water or olive oil.

- **LAMINATE**: A composite material made of plastic-coated paper (heat resistant paper-melamine). Common brand names of laminate are Arborite and Formica. **Advantages**: Inexpensive, easy to maintain. Huge variety of colors available. **Disadvantages**: Not scratch resistant and difficult to repair if damaged. Hot pots cannot be set on counters. **Note**: Use soap and water to clean.

- **WOOD (BUTCHER BLOCK)**: Natural and warm in appearance, this classic fibrous substance is often made with hardwoods glued into strips. **Advantages**: Can use as a cutting board. Damaged surfaces may be sanded and resealed with oil or varnish. **Disadvantages**: Absorbs liquids. Not heat resistant. Turns black if exposed to large quantities of water (sealing will deter color change). **Note**: Butcher block may be used as a portion of the counter instead of the entire counter.

- **CERAMIC TILE**: Made by fusing together glass and clay. **Advantages**: Heat, burn resistant. Somewhat stain and scratch, mold/mildew resistant. Waterproof. **Disadvantages**: Needs to be maintained regularly. Grout must be sealed for best results.

- **CONCRETE**: **Advantages**: The cost of a concrete countertop can be lessened by pouring and installing the concrete on your own. The sink and counter may be cast all-in-one. Easy to shape and paint. Heat and scratch resistant. **Disadvantages**: Cutting on concrete surface, will dull knives. May crack; absorbs liquids. Acids will etch surface, should be sealed and may need waxing to repel stains. **Note**: Wash with soap and water. Use a poultice to remove stains; do not wipe with glass cleaner. Fix cracks with epoxy filler. Buff out white spots (that appear to be water spots) with 800 grit sandpaper.

- **SLATE**: A fabulous natural stone quarried all over the world. High silica content is key for slate countertops. **Advantages**: Good-quality slate has a low absorption rate making it stain resistant. May or may not need sealing and can withstand direct heat. Does not react with acids. Not likely to harbor bacteria. **Disadvantages**: Research required, not all slate is equal, some streak and show white marks; may stain, discolor, scratch and flake. Some slates are soft and absorb wetness. **Note**: Apply a thin layer of mineral oil following installation. Wash with soap and water.

- **LIMESTONE**: An extremely heavy natural material, this stone is almost as hard as granite. **Advantage**: Some are scratch resistant. **Disadvantage**: Due to the weight, installation is challenging. Limited chemical and stain resistance, sealing will help. **Note**: Use a poultice to absorb stains, either hydrogen peroxide or acetone.

- **TERRAZZO**: A man-made stone composed of chips that are mixed with cement and then polished. Care is similar to marble. **Advantages**: Does not stain easily. A wide selection of colors, polishes and textures. **Disadvantages**: Needs protection from absorption. Sealing product regularly will reduce etching and increase resistant to stains and scratches.

Tip: To prevent coffee cans from staining counters/cupboard shelves with rust, ring stains; save a lid from an old coffee can and place it under the can in use.

Carpet Ideas That You Can't Beat

- Old-fashioned beating is the best method for cleaning an area rug. Use a broom handle, strong stick or old tennis racket to hit the rug several times on each side (only to be done in dry weather).

- When an area rug is first unrolled it may have a tendency to bulge. Remove these bumps by using a broom handle. Start at the center and push half of the wrinkle to the left. Push the other half of the wrinkle to the right. Your carpet should now be smooth (too bad this doesn't work on humans). **Note:** Never push the entire wrinkle to one side because that can stretch the rug improperly.

- Sprouts are loose pieces of yarn often found on new carpets; this is not an indication of poor quality. The yarn should be carefully clipped, NOT pulled.

- Frequently rotate your carpet to equalize any sun damage. Close window shades, shutters or curtains to protect area rugs.

- It is good to vacuum area rugs regularly, but be gentle. Avoid a power brush or "beater bar," these can cause "raking" (an effect that leaves the carpet fibers standing up in certain areas). Also, to clean fringes remove the attachment and run the nozzle across the fringe.
  Tip: Be careful when positioning plants on an area rug. If leakage has already occurred see the "Fantastic Stain Removal Recipe for Carpets" from *Household Solutions 1 with Substitutions,* page 46.

- Area rugs should be profession- ally cleaned every 3-5 years (depending on the amount of traffic).

- You can extend the life of an area rug by placing good- quality padding underneath the rug; this allows the fibers to breath.

- When choosing an area rug consider the following:
  - ◆ How much traffic will the rug get? The denser the pile, the better your rug will wear. Nylon, polypropylene, polyester and acrylic are fairly easy to clean.
  - ◆ Choose a rug that picks up the colors of your furnishings. Elements of a rug pattern can be further incorporated into the overall design scheme.
  - ◆ Light colors make a room look bigger. Dark colors give a warm cozy effect.

- To repair broken braids on a braided rug, use a whipstitch to prevent further damage. Start just before the damaged area and stitch the braids together. Extend the stitches just beyond the damaged area and secure the knot.

- When a rug is to be stored for more than a few months: clean it, spray with insecticide, wrap in plastic wrap or Tyvek paper. **Note:** Do not use newspaper, brown paper or mothballs.

- Latex-backed rugs (this includes most hand-hooked rugs) must not be cleaned with petroleum-based solvents.

- What determines price points for area rugs? Machine-made vs. handmade, synthetic vs. natural fibers and size are all determining factors. Woven, tufted, bordered, sculptured, textured, also Oriental, Berber and Native American designs can be found in nearly any price range.

- Currently, wool as well as rayon and cotton are the most commonly used textiles for area rugs. Rug designs are divided into 2 categories – rectilinear (geometric) and curvilinear (organic). Organic motifs tend to be more complex than geometric patterns.

- When you compile a list of precious household items, remember that quality oriental rugs, especially those woven out of fine silk, are as valuable as any other specialized art form. Even very small silk rugs can be worth thousands of dollars.

Choosing the Right Wood Finish

The finishes on the market have come a long way, your lifestyle and specific needs will dictate the best products for your home.

- The following tricks will help you determine what type of finish is currently on a floor or piece of furniture. If the wood was installed or the furniture built before 1965 you can assume the finish used was **varnish or shellac**. Using a coin, scratch the surface in an inconspicuous area. If the finish flakes, it is likely shellac or varnish. Also, moisten a rag with denatured alcohol and rub on a hidden area. If the finish turns gummy it is shellac. Next, check for wax finish (in an inconspicuous area), apply 2 drops of water, if within 10 minutes white spots appear, the floor has a wax finish. To remove the white spots, rub with fine steel wool impregnated with wax.

- **Shellac** is an organic, natural finish. It is created by combining the excrement of the lac bug with denatured alcohol. Shellac is susceptible to water spotting, therefore it is not recommended on kitchen or bathroom floors. Shellac is an excellent barrier in protecting wood from humidity. At present, shellac and varnishes are used much less than in the past because they require full sanding before application.

- The difference between **lacquer and shellac** is that lacquer is a man-made finish developed after WW I. It is usually applied with a spray gun and is widely used on furniture, however, it may strip paint. It is best to apply lacquer over another kind of clear coat or paint. Shellac is more flexible and less hard than lacquer and can be brushed or sprayed on. Consider cold-cure lacquer if you want a very glossy black or white finish. **Note:** Shellac is the only FDA-approved finish for children's toys.

- The difference between **varnish and shellac** is that varnish is harder than shellac, making touch-ups more difficult. Varnish can be brushed several times during application, while shellac dries faster and has a tendency to lap mark and dribble (meaning application must be fast). Shellac repair is easier than varnish repair, however, varnish is not as durable as some of the newer finishes. When using varnish, use three coats, allowing each coat to dry overnight with light sanding and vacuuming between coats.

- Linseed oil, oil varnishes and some urethanes react with air to produce a film finish that is more durable than shellac. This gives a strong finish, making it difficult for water and chemicals to penetrate.

- Good-quality urethane has UV blockers (check the label). As well, good-quality water-based urethanes do not yellow (apply 4 coats). This finish is durable, has a mild odor, is fast drying, non-combustible, and is available in satin to gloss finish. **Disadvantages**: water-based urethane is typically more expensive than oil and the finish is not as thick looking. Urethane appears milky but goes on clear. **Note**: Read the label for recommended use and make sure the product says, "Non-Yellowing"!

- Polyurethane oil-based finishes are moisture resistant and some of the most scratch-resistant products available. Oil-based polyurethane is durable, has a moderate odor, is slow to dry and is combustible. It is hard to touch-up and may darken the wood with age; it is available in satin to gloss finish. Apply 3 coats, leaving each coat to dry overnight with light sanding and vacuuming between coats.

- The words polyurethane and urethane are interchangeable. The term polyurethane came about because the predominant chemical group present in the polymer was the urethane group. Polyurethane products are durable, non-marking: oil, solvent, mold, fungus and water-resistant. **Note**: A solvent-based urethane has oil components that are used as part of the chemical makeup of the polyurethane finish. Dry time is 24 hours.

- Wax or oil finishes are durable, shiny, have a mild odor, are combustible and may leave water spots. **Note**: Do not wax a urethane-finished floor; doing so will cause the wood to become slippery, requiring continuous waxing as maintenance.

- Add shine to old indoor wood furniture. Begin by sealing the wood with a clear varnish then apply a wax finish, (Carnauba, Bri-wax and beeswax are good choices). **Caution**: Select the best wax for your project and read the label. Some commercial wax or polishes can reduce the luster of your finish and create a film, which will require extensive refinishing.

- Before choosing a finish, decide whether you want a matte, satin or gloss look. Exterior grade varnish has the best water resistance. Marine grade is designed to resist salt. Satin or semi-gloss finishes show traffic patterns less than gloss. **Note**: Always apply any brush-on finish with a very good-quality brush.

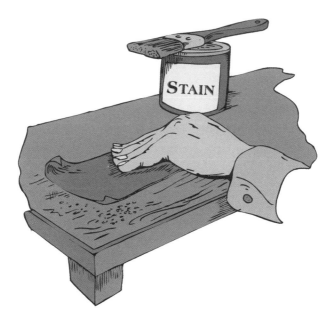

- Oil-based finishes bring out the natural color of wood. Water-based finishes leave the wood lighter than oil and have a tendency to reduce the natural color variations of the grain.

- There are a few different options for **stripping wood surfaces**: UV strippers, sanding and chemical strippers. If a floor has been sanded often it may be too thin to be sanded again. If this is the case, chemical removal is a good option (ventilation is important).

- Use an old deck of cards to help remove an old finish. Apply the solvent according to the manufacturer's directions; when the solvent bubbles, scrape the area with one card after another instead of using a sharp blade.

- **To refinish oak cabinets**: Rub with super-fine steel wool and contact cement solvent. Wash with all-purpose cleaner and apply 2 coats of urethane. **Note**: Remove grease on cupboards by applying car wax and buffing.

- **Polyurethaned palms**: Remove polyurethane from fingers by smearing them with peanut butter. Wash as normal.

- To avoid disappointment, whatever the project, read product labels to determine recommended uses.

Ways to Create a Wallpaper Statement

- Liven up your world with wallpaper. There are several exciting possibilities, wallpaper is affordable, easy to install, coordinates with the looks you love and can add value to your house (or office) while setting a mood.

- Supplies: large table, step ladder, tape measure, pencil, scissors, string, chalk, level, screwdriver, plastic bucket, sponge, rags, smoothing brush, paint roller, tray for adhesive (for unpasted paper), utility knife, seam roller, adhesive and premixed drywall patch (to repair damaged walls).

- **To remove wallpaper** there are a variety of options:
  - **Chemical wallpaper remover**: Make criss-cross slits so the chemical can soak in. Follow manufacturer's instructions.
  - **Steamer**: Only heat a small area at a time. Keep the steamer a good distance away from your body.
  - **My favorite**: Use a handsaw or utility knife to score the wallpaper. Mix ⅓ cup (75 mL) fabric softener, ⅔ cup (150 mL) hot water or 1 cup (250 mL) vinegar with 1 gallon (4 L) hot water. Pour into a spray bottle to moisten paper. Leave for 15 minutes before peeling.
  - Apply TSP (Trisodium Phosphate); wear gloves.

Save newspapers and use them to remove old wallpaper. Score the wallpaper with a utility knife. Mix 1 part vinegar to 3 parts water. Dip several large sheets of newspaper into the solution and press them against the wall so they stick. Wait 1 hour and remove, the wallpaper should peel right off.

- Prepare walls before installation to ensure that the paper adheres correctly. Clean walls, sanding rough surfaces. **Tip**: When patching holes do not use an oil-based product, it can bleed through wall covering. It takes 24-48 hours for wallpaper to set and there is significant movement as the paper contracts. If it hasn't formed a good bond, it will pull away from the wall. Preparing the wall properly also ensures that when the paper is removed it is less likely to damage the wall.

Make your own **Wallpaper Glue**: Combine 1½ cups (375 mL) flour with ½ cup (125 mL) sugar. Slowly, add 1 cup (250 mL) cold water and mix until smooth. Stir in 2 cups (500 mL) boiling water and heat. When firm, remove from heat and add 1 tbsp. (15 mL) alum. Store in an airtight container for up to 4 weeks. Add water if paste hardens.

- When wallpapering, to estimate how much wallpaper you will need, calculate the square footage of the room then add 15% for waste.

- When applying wallpaper in areas where dampness or steam tend to occur, paint shellac over the joints and edges to prevent the paper from peeling. **Tip**: To keep grease spots on old wallpaper from soaking through to new wallpaper, paint the spots with shellac before applying the new paper.

- New vinyl wallpaper needs to be scored before installation by applying the wet solution, so the solution has a means to penetrate the paper.

- To determine where you want the pattern to fall at the ceiling line, hold an unrolled roll against the wall. On the back, mark the spot where to begin. When cutting the first strip leave a couple of inches (5 cm) at the top and bottom for trimming. **Tip**: Hanging a wallpaper border at the ceiling will give a room height. To make a room more inviting and comfortable, place the border at chair rail height.

- Leftover wallpaper? Line shelves and drawers, wrap gifts; frame as artwork; laminate wallpaper and use as placemats (also works well for kids' rooms craft table); decorate parcels by cutting paper into strips to make ribbon, curl edges using scissors; make book covers.

- Before cleaning wallpaper, find out if it is washable. Test on an inconspicuous area first; if the color runs, bleeds or fades it is not washable. Fabric wallpaper should be vacuumed regularly using a soft brush.

- To clean fingerprints on wallpaper, gently rub the area with stale bread or use a clean plastic sponge dipped in baby powder. **Tip**: An art eraser also works well to remove marks from the walls.

- To remove grease or crayon marks from wallpaper, quickly blot the area. Cover with a clean paper towel and press with a warm iron to soak up the grease. Next, wash the area with Dawn dish soap and a plastic scouring pad. **Tip**: WD-40 also works to remove crayon and grease from wallpaper. Be careful not to rip the paper and test a sample before applying WD-40 to wallpaper.

 Hair spray on wallpaper will disappear if you wash the area with a mixture of 1 cup (250 mL) fabric softener and ⅔ cup (150 mL) cool water.

- If you need to patch wallpaper, never cut a scrap piece. Always use a piece that you have torn by hand, tear toward the wrong side of the wallpaper to make the patch nearly invisible.

Ideas That Mirror Your Home

- Prevent bathroom mirrors from fogging up by wiping shaving cream, rubbing alcohol, glycerin or Dawn dish soap over the glass. This will last for several weeks or until you clean the bathroom (whichever comes first).

- When using a glass cleaner, spray the cleaner on a clean cloth, not directly onto the mirror surface. It is important to keep the frame dry, also prolonged moisture around the edges can damage the mirror backing.

- If the mirror backing begins to wear off, tape shiny pieces of aluminum foil over the damaged spots to draw attention away from them. **Note**: Antique mirrors often have worn areas which add to their appearance.

The easiest way to clean a mirror is by using 3-day-old or older newspaper and water or, my personal favorite, microfiber cloths. Add a few drops of vinegar for added shine. **Tip**: In cases where mirrors are extremely dirty, combine ½ cup (125 mL) ammonia, ½ cup (125 mL) vinegar and 1 gallon (4 L) of water. Rinse with a clear vinegar solution and wipe with newspaper. Or collect tea-leaves in a bucket to clean windows, glass and mirrors. Cover leaves with rainwater and leave overnight. Strain and use the cold "tea" with a squeegee. Dry with 3-day-old or older newspaper.

- Keep mirrors from steaming up. Fill tub with 2" (5 cm) cold water then gradually add hot or warm water to the tub.

- To remove hair spray on mirrors, apply vinegar or liquid fabric softener in 2 cups (500 mL) water. Dry with 3-day-old or older newspaper.

- To avoid streaks on windows, clean them on gloomy days or in the morning before the sun beams in.

- Use unframed bevel-edged mirrors as placemats or under a centerpiece for a formal meal. Or place mirrors under dishes on a buffet table.

- When transporting a mirror or a glass-fronted painting, put packing tape across the front of the mirror/glass in an "X" pattern to keep the glass securely positioned in case it breaks. Wrap in bubble wrap or blank newsprint with cardboard and packing taped around the sides. Fill loose spaces with wadded paper. Put in a flat box, seal and mark, "FRAGILE – MIRROR." **Tip**: To remove stuck on tape, spray on household superstar WD-40.

- Remove paint splatters from a mirror by gently rubbing the area with a razor blade. If the surface is stained combine and apply tea, water and detergent; wipe with fine steel wool. **Tip**: Be sure to wear work gloves when handling unframed mirror.

- Avoid installing mirrors that fit too tightly because they will accentuate surrounding walls that are not perfectly square. **Tip**: If you cannot find the appropriately sized mirror for a wall you can have one custom-cut.

- Grouping mirrors together presents an interesting focal point to a room in the same way as grouping a variety of photo frames.

- When purchasing a mirror, choose ¼" (6 mm) thick as apposed to ⅛" (3 mm) thick, which tends to distort the reflection.

- Eliminate water spots on a mirror by drying it with a dryer sheet.

- Choose a beveled over flat mirror because it has a more traditional and elegant appearance.

- Hang mirrors on a wall directly opposite a window. The reflected outdoor view will give the illusion of a second window in the room. If you hang 2 mirrors directly opposite one another in an entryway, hallway or small room you can create the illusion of infinity.

- Put a mirror on the ceiling of a medicine cabinet so that you can see what is on the top shelf.

- A floor-to-ceiling mirror on both sides of a fireplace gives a dark cramped living area a feeling of space.

MIRROR TRIVIA:

If you are ever stuck in the wild and don't have a mirror, what can you use as a substitute to signal for help?

ANSWER: Bottom of a tin plate, blade of a knife, belt buckle, compact disc, binocular lens, polished connector sleeve of a tent pole. If you have none of the above on hand, use your cell phone.

Pointers for Combining Pattern and Color

The purest and most thoughtful minds are those which love color the most.
   – John Ruskin

- The color palette is the most important aspect of using pattern. If all the patterns are in the same color palette, the patterns will probably go together well. The colors do not need to match exactly but should be similar.

- Start with a solid backdrop and layer textures, colors and patterns on top. Before selecting large prints remember that a little bit goes a long way, e.g., throw pillows and valances.

- When choosing solid colors, consider draping large pieces in a room with heavy cottons, linens, velvets, chenilles and silks. These are practical choices for the main solid.

- Create contrast by adding a few items of a different color, but make sure that they do not break the visual harmony of the décor. Combine small, large and textured prints. Little hits of pattern make wonderful accents. Use mini prints like checks, tweeds, toiles, florals and hounds tooth for throw pillows, window treatments and bed skirts.

- Textured solids give a room richness and depth. If decorating a room in a neutral scheme the textured solid can be a different shade from the solid fabric. Use textures in large pillows or shams, e.g., quilted silk, embroidered weaves, damasks, raffia.

- If you want your house to look like a classic showpiece, combine styles by blending periods that complement each other, e.g., French and Rococo, English Renaissance and Victorian, Queen Anne and Chippendale, Neoclassic and Empire.

- The color palette of the popular Victorian style varies, however, pictures are often seen mounted with heavy frames and dark mats. Also, for Victorian homes incorporate mahogany and cherry woods into furniture. Accents are key. Wall décor can vary from still life, botanicals, nature and religion.

- Unless the fabric patterns are subtle or muted try to limit the number of patterns in one room to four or fewer.

- Another popular style is known as English Cottage. Flowery fabrics are combined with soft shades and bright touches. Wood is typically painted white and the room usually incorporates at least 2 patterns of similar colors.

- Vary the style of fabric patterns. Instead of using 3 plaids try a floral, plaid and stripe or you could add checks or a geometric pattern.

- Alternate the scale of the pattern. If you have a large plaid fabric select small-scale floral and a medium-scale stripe. Use small-scale fabric patterns in a smaller room. In larger rooms, where pieces are viewed from a distance, these tend to be seen as a texture or solid.

- Don't cluster the fabrics in one area of the room. Spread them out to give visual balance. Fabrics should complement each other.

- When choosing a carpet to match a design take note, if the carpet has a geometric pattern, e.g., a trellis, then choose the opposite, e.g., a floral, for the wallpaper. If the carpet is a floral choose the opposite, such as a stripe, for wallpaper.

- Combining traditional with contemporary design is impressive when executed properly. A traditional-style home with just a few select contemporary pieces makes for an eye-appealing look. The "shock" of a very contemporary piece in a room of traditional furnishings creates surprise and interest.

- Southwest and Western Style tend to be lumped into one category but there are differences. The Western theme showcases cowboys, horses, boots and saddles. The color palette includes bright shades of orange, red and purple that are depicted in sunsets. Also, rustic leather or denim with rough wood textures are accessorized with deer antlers, saddle blanket rugs, animal pictures. On the other hand, Southwest Style focuses on desert landscapes combined with simplified Spanish or Mexican furnishings. The color palette includes soft earth and sky tones, terra cotta, teal, purple and green.

Coffee Table Secrets

Coffee tables have a special place in our hearts, we gather around them to visit with family and friends, play games and display treasured possessions.

- Be cautious when purchasing furniture. Solid wood may mean particleboard and/or MDF (medium-density fiberboard). These will not last under heavy use. Always ask specifically what kind of wood was used. Solid oak, cherry, mahogany or ash are great choices.

- To finish an unfinished coffee table, the toughest seal is a polyurethane varnish. This contains alkyd resins, polyurethane plastics and additives to help it dry and create an almost bulletproof plastic barrier. **Note:** Water-based polyurethane has several advantages over oil-based: it has less dry time; it is self-leveling (to create a smooth surface); it is nearly odorless and easy to clean up.

- The following solutions will help remedy water damage on wood:
  - Soak cheesecloth with hot water and 3 drops of ammonia. Rub the wood and then go over the entire area with a soft oiled cloth.
  - Use an organic stripper and stripping pad. Wash and apply wood bleach. Apply a solvent-based urethane stain to refinish.
  - Sand and refinish.

- Burns on a wooden table may be permanent and noticeable depending on the depth of the burn. The following suggestions may help:
  - Make a paste using baking soda and vinegar, let sit for 15 minutes then wipe off.
  - Wipe the area using a pencil eraser.
  - Patch with wood stain.

- Wipe scratches on a coffee table with mineral oil. Remove excess.

- To remove dark rings on a wooden coffee table, sand and then mix oxalic acid with water until crystals will no longer dissolve. Apply with a synthetic brush until wet. Leave to dry. Rinse with water, then sand and finish. Do this outdoors and wear a mask.

- If the drawers on your wooden coffee table are sticky, rub clear Bri-wax or other paste wax on the edges, a candle also works well. This will make a huge difference unless the drawer is in need of repair.

- To determine the appropriate coffee table size, allow a minimum of 15" (38 cm) between the edge of the couch and the coffee table.

- The standard height of a coffee table is 16" (41 cm). If eating at it, 25" (63.5 cm) is best. Modern coffee tables can be as low as 11" (28 cm). Typically, coffee tables should be the same height as the chair seats in the room.

- If you cannot locate the perfect coffee table, consider having one custom built by a skilled craftsperson. That way you won't have to settle.

- Add a unique aspect to your living space by investing in a multi-function coffee table. New on the market are acrylic-seal fish-tank tables; these come with a complete lighting kit and filters. Adjustable-height tables, removable-tray tables and tables that double as chess or other game surfaces are also popular.

- Glass tops can protect wooden tables but moisture may get trapped between the glass and wood. Use rubber bumpers (available at most glass shops) to create an air space, thus allowing the wood to breathe.

- Use a computer vacuum attachment or an air compressor, to clean hard to reach crevices on a glass-top coffee table.

- Select a decorative object or collection of objects for the tabletop, e.g., a vase of flowers, blown glass bowl, candle grouping or a collection of coffee-table books. Be sure to leave at least enough space for a coffee cup.

- Scratches and worn areas of wood coffee tables can be salvages by applying a small amount of wax with fine steel wool to the scratched area. Apply the wax in the same direction as the grain.

SCIENCE TRIVIA:

If you screamed continuously for 8 years, 7 months and 6 days you would produce enough energy to heat a cup of coffee (to put on your coffee table). See how it all comes back to the coffee table?

Tricky Fabric Stains

- After purchasing new towels, wash them separately 4-5 times before putting them in with other loads, because residual dyes may ruin clothes. **Tip**: Using fabric softener when drying towels makes them less absorbent. For fluffier towels, do not dry them completely after washing.

- **Small White Marks on Towels**: These are bleach spots that are likely caused by whitening agents in toothpastes, creams and soaps. **Tip**: If you have a pull on a towel, cut it off. Pulling it will ruin the fabric.

- **Egg Stains on Clothing**: Scrape away as much egg as possible. Sponge with cold water. Never use hot water as heat sets the stain. If this does not succeed, spread the stain with a paste of cream of tartar, water and a crushed Aspirin. Leave for 20-30 minutes. Rinse well in warm water.

- **Ring Around the Collar**: Dirty neck rings on shirts can be cleaned using shampoo which is made with surfactants specifically created to clean away oils, i.e., body oils. Apply shampoo to collar and scrub, rubbing gently as you would wash your hair; launder as usual.

- **Ink Stains on Leather Upholstery**: According to Fibernew Industries in Winnipeg, leather owners are advised to wash blue jeans several times before sitting on leather furniture to avoid blue dye stains. Also, keep leather away from direct sunlight and apply a car or leather conditioner on a regular basis so the leather remains soft and supple. Do not clean leather with dishwashing soap or Windex, as it tends to lighten the color over time.

- **Tar**: Spray WD-40 onto stain. Let sit for 10 minutes Wash as usual. May require extensive blotting. Or, dab with turpentine or unsalted butter. Treat the area with degreaser and wash normally; the stain may take more than 1 washing to vanish.

 Hair Dye on Clothing: **Immediately** spray with hair spray to keep the dye from spreading. Wash as soon as possible with 1 tbsp. (15 mL) ammonia and 1 cup (250 mL) water. This is a difficult stain so act quickly.

- **Tree Sap**: Remove by applying one of the following: Dawn dish soap, rubbing alcohol, peanut butter, baking soda, washing soda, WD-40 or butter. Wash as usual.

Yellowed Baptismal Gown: (Caused by oxidation.) Soak overnight in ½ cup (125 mL) heavy-duty detergent and 1 gallon (4 L) water or 1 cup (125 mL) washing soda and 8 cups (2 L) water. Rinse 3 times. Repeat if still yellowed or dry clean.

- **Carpet Stains**: Use baby wipes to remove carpet stains. They also work on spills such as blood, ketchup and motor oil.

- **Grease Stains**: Spray automotive degreaser on tough grease stains, but don't leave the degreaser on the fabric stain for more than 15 minutes before washing in hot water because the degreaser will become ineffective.

- **Lint**: To prevent sweaters from collecting lint, use fabric softener in the wash or toss a pair of old pantihose into the dryer to attract lint. **Tip**: Clean hair and lint from clothing or upholstery by wrapping your hands with masking tape and patting the surface.

- **Newspaper Ink**: To remove newspaper ink stains, pre-treat the marked area with "Shout" before washing. Examine clothing to make sure that the stain is gone before putting it in the dryer.

Perspiration Stains: Get tough. Remove perspiration stains from clothes with 1 part vinegar in 4 parts water. Rinse. Also, soak socks in vinegar to get rid of odor (do not rinse). Or, combine ½ cup (125 mL) washing soda and 4 cups (1 L) water in a stainless steel pot and boil shirts to get rid of stain on cotton. **Tip 1**: To avoid perspiration stains on fabric switch to plain deodorant. **Tip 2**: To get rid of perspiration odors soak clothes in mouthwash. Or, use Aspirin to remove perspiration stains from clothing. Dissolve 8-10 aspirins in a glass of water. Soak the stain in the water for 30 minutes. The acid from the Aspirin dissolves the perspiration stains. Launder as usual.

- **Graffiti on Bathroom Walls**: Spray with hairspray, wipe immediately.

Do Away with Mildew

 Remove Mildew from Wood Patio Furniture: Combine 1 cup (250 mL) ammonia, ½ cup (125 mL) vinegar, ¼ cup (60 mL) baking soda and 1 gallon (4 L) of water. Wipe on furniture and rinse.

- Dirt on hard surfaces such as paint, tile or wood resembles the discoloration caused by mildew. To determine if the spot is dirt or mildew, use a cotton swab to apply a drop of chlorine bleach on the surface, mildew will be bleached within 2 minutes. Dirt will not bleach.

- Clean mildew from around the tub area by placing cotton balls soaked with bleach or vinegar in each corner. Clean the inside of the tub as normal. Remove cotton balls from corners and rinse.

- Discourage mildew by leaving the shower door or curtain open after a shower. Before getting into the shower, spray the inside with mildew cleaner. Scrub while you shower.

- **Mildew on Grout**: Apply bleach with an old toothbrush to remove the mildew color. After cleaning the grout with bleach rinse with water.

 To get **Shower Curtains** really clean: Add 1 cup (250 mL) vinegar to the water when laundering.

- Garments with mildew spots should be soaked in vinegar for several hours before laundering.

- Keep closets dry to protect clothes from mildew. Tie several pieces of chalk together and hang them from a hook inside the closet.

- In a closed space such as a closet, mildew can be controlled. Use a continuously burning 60-watt bulb in a large closet to raise the temperature (which in turn lowers humidity). Use smaller bulb in a smaller enclosure.

 To Clean Mildew on Carpets: Vacuum the carpet and throw away the bag. Combine ½ tsp. (2 mL) liquid dishwashing detergent with 1 cup (250 mL) warm water. Sponge onto the area and let sit for 10 minutes. Rinse and blot with white paper towels. Then, combine 2 tbsp. (30 mL) ammonia with 1 cup (250 mL) warm water. Blot area with white paper towels. Air dry.

- Prevent mildew by spraying an antibacterial product on the damp side of wallpaper before hanging it.

- Remove excess moisture with constant air movement and good ventilation. When the air outside is drier than inside, ventilation lets dry air

enter, pick up moisture and carry it outside. When normal breezes are not sufficient you can use electric fans placed in a window, set in a wall or vented to the attic to move air.

- Cool air holds less moisture than warm air. One of the benefits of an installed air-conditioning system is that it removes moisture from the air by taking up warm air, cooling it and circulating the cool, dry air back into the room. **Tip**: Attach a humidistat to the unit to control the humidity.

 Mildew Inside a Tent: Can be scrubbed with 1 tsp. (5 mL) detergent-free soap combined with 1 cup (250 mL) water. Next, sponge the tent with disinfectant and air out the canvas.

- Put newspaper under car mats in snowy weather to absorb moisture.

Are all Bacteria Bad?

According to the Soap and Detergent Association, "more than 75% of liquid soap and more than 25% of bar soaps on supermarket shelves contain a product called, Triclosan, an antibiotic that kills most bacteria, both good and bad". Triclosan is a chemical that is known for its antibacterial properties, and is an ingredient in many detergents, dishwashing liquids, soaps, deodorants, kitchen sponges, fabrics, cosmetics, some toothpastes, lotions, creams and insect repellents. Over the last few years the safety of Triclosan has been debated. Companies that manufacture products containing Triclosan say that there are no health risks but the United States Environmental Protection Agency (EPA) has registered it as a pesticide. Some say that killing off too many bacteria can lead to a new problem called "Super bugs" (bacteria that Triclosan cannot kill), others disagree. Whether we are purchasing products for consumption, cleaning or cosmetics be careful. Even when we know what goes into a product we are often not aware of how it is made, which can also affect product safety.

The moral of the story? Variety, instead of being brand loyal and sticking to the same products over and over again, unless the product is completely organic, mix things up. In terms of foods, cosmetics, detergents, cleaners, etc. That way, if you are using products that are in some way unhealthy, you won't be consuming too much of one thing.

Odors – The Nose Knows Best

- **Antique Wood Furniture, Drawers, Cupboards and Coffee Tables**: Lingering odors on newly stained wood can be remedied by rubbing the surface with a deodorant stick. Polish with a soft cloth. Freshen up furniture by soaking a slice of white bread in vinegar. Put the bread into a dish and place inside the furniture. Kitty litter, charcoal, crumpled-up newspaper and coffee grounds are also effective!

- **Wooden Coffee Table, Musty Smell**: Turn the table upside down and sprinkle with coffee grounds. Cover the grounds with plastic wrap and tape the sides. Leave for several days.

- **Microwave**: Food burnt in the microwave, e.g., popcorn, has an odor that lingers. Combine lemon slices, vinegar, vanilla, dish soap and water, or baking soda with water; heat in the microwave until the liquid boils over. Wipe the surface. Another option is to unplug the microwave and fill it with crumpled-up newspaper, coffee grounds or a bowl of charcoal. Leave for a few days to absorb odors.

- **Automobile Odors**: Open windows and spray with "Outstanding Homemade Air Freshener," page 80; sprinkle baking soda in car ashtrays; tuck fabric softener sheets under seats and place pads of newspaper beneath car mats; place 3 or 4 halved fresh apples or charcoal in an open container.

- **Refrigerators/Freezers**: Clean refrigerator with baking soda or vinegar and water. Set out charcoal or a halved raw potato to absorb odors. Coffee grounds placed in a bowl or sprinkled along the bottom of the fridge is effective; this also works for musty areas such as old boxes.

- **Extreme Fridge and Sports Bag Nightmare**: Remove all contents and stuff, stuff, STUFF with crumpled-up newspaper. Leave for a week. Or, make **Hockey Pucks**: Melt paraffin wax in a pot, drop in 1 tsp. (5 mL) tea tree oil. Pour into muffin cups. Let cool and place in hockey bags. **Note**: Many pieces of sports equipment are washable. Check care labels.

- **Books**: For musty smelling books, freeze them for 24 hours, take them out and position them standing up and fanned open. Also, slide a fabric softener sheet or old newspaper between a few pages. Or seal books overnight in a container of cat litter. Or sprinkle baby powder between pages. Clean books by vacuuming them.

- **Cutting Boards**: Sprinkle lemon juice or vinegar on cutting boards and scrub with an abrasive cloth. Rinse.

Pet Odors on Carpets: Put cotton balls soaked with your favorite fragrance into the vacuum cleaner bag. Or, in a spray bottle, combine 6 drops of cedar wood, 3 drops of tea tree oil or enough water to fill the bottle. Spray on fabrics and carpet.

- **Fabric/Mattress**: Combat smells by combining 1 part vodka with 1 part water; spray on fabric. Or sprinkle a generous amount of borax or baking soda on mattresses to kill odor; place 3-4 dryer sheets under bed sheets.

- **Plastic Storage Containers**: Mix vanilla and water in the container and leave for 12 hours (also works inside fridge). Or pack with crumpled newspaper, close the lid and leave for 3 days or freeze container. **Tip**: To remove tomato-related stains in plastic containers, leave in the sun for a couple of hours.

- **Fingers**: Strong smells such as automotive degreaser, WD-40, turpentine, bleach or nail polish remover can be tamed by a rubbing stick deodorant or toothpaste onto fingers.

Outstanding Homemade Air Freshener: While it is true that fabric softener is made with chemicals that are potentially hazardous when used in large amounts, the following recipe may be used in moderation. This inexpensive, easy-to-make mixture can give you the same scent as commercial sprays. In a spray bottle combine: 2 cups (500 mL) of your favorite liquid fabric softener with 4 cups (1 L) water. The amount of fabric softener may be greatly reduced depending on your desire for fragrance intensity.

Air Freshener: Combine ½ cup (125 mL) crushed bay leaves, ¼ cup (60 mL) dried sage and 1 cup (250 mL) witch hazel. Let sit at room temperature for 3 days. Strain and transfer remaining liquid to a spray bottle.

Room Deodorizer Mist Spray: Add 30-50 drops of any essential oil to an 8 oz. (250 mL) spray bottle. Fill remainder with distilled water. Glass bottles are best because essential oils will erode plastic over time. OR, drop tea tree oil into an open, full bottle of vinegar and set the open container behind the toilet. Caution: with children and pets.

 Jelly-O Deodorizer: Combine 4-serving size (84 g) package of any Jell-o flavor, ¾ cup (175 mL) boiling water, 2 tbsp. (30 mL) vodka and 5 drops of any essential oil. Pour mixture into clean glass jars, and place open jars in bathrooms, closets, kitchens, cars, etc.

 Create-a-Smile Air Freshener: In a saucepan, heat 8 oz. (250 mL) concentrated liquid potpourri until almost boiling. Remove from heat; slowly add 1 envelope , (1 tbsp./15 mL) clear gelatin and 1 tsp. (5 mL) salt. Pour another 8 oz. (250 mL) liquid potpourri into the pan and add your favorite essential oils. Fill baby food jars with mixture and once cooled tuck into closets, lockers, behind toilets, on shelves in the living room or kitchen.

- Most people know that placing a box of baking soda in the freezer will keep ice cubes from tasting funny. But did you know that wiping out an empty, unplugged freezer with vinegar and standing a bowl of vinegar on the bottom is also a great way to kill odors?

- **Bathroom Odors**: Keep an open box of baking soda behind the toilet to absorb bathroom odors. Or, for a more decorative presentation, put baking soda into a glass container and mix with bath salts.

- **Fireplace Soot Odor**: To reduce the smell of soot after cleaning out ashes, place a shallow pan of baking soda inside the fireplace and leave overnight.

 Smoke Smell on Walls: In a spray bottle, combine 1 gallon (4 L) water, ¼ cup (60 mL) ammonia, ¼ cup (60 mL) vinegar and ¼ cup (60 mL) washing soda. Spray on walls, let sit 10 minutes; rinse. Or, set out bowls of vinegar, charcoal or baking powder to absorb the smell.

- **Smelly Shoes**: Help is on the way – place tea leaves in a pair of knee-high pantihose and stuff into shoes. Let sit for 1-2 days; the smell will disappear.

- Don't throw away used green tea leaves; they work well to mask odors in kitty litter. Also, place used green tea leaves in an uncovered bowl in the refrigerator to absorb odors (they eat odors for up to 3 days) then sprinkle the leaves around plants to add nutrients. Rub hands with wet green tea leaves as a deodorizer after cutting onions or garlic.

Hi Reena,

Recently my dad gave me an old trunk full of dress-up clothes. At some point there were mothballs in the trunk, so all the clothes smell like mothballs. I tried washing it with 1 cup of vinegar, as well as spraying with Febreze. No luck. Any suggestions. Thanks. Linda

Hi Linda,

Getting rid of the smell of mothballs takes time, remember it is a pesticide and must work its way out of the fibers. Best solution is to hang the clothing outside for a few weeks. Depending on what the fabric is, falling snow may be extremely helpful in absorbing the odor, as is the sun. After bringing the clothing inside, soak them in a stainless steel pot with washing soda and water or baking soda and water for 1 hour. Then toss the washing soda and water mixture into the washing machine, wash as usual. Thanks for the question Linda!

Hi Reena,

My grandmother left me a beautiful brass candelabra. How do I clean it? Thanks, Carol

Hi Carol,

There are several ways to clean brass.

First, determine if the item is actually brass or brass plated. If a magnet connects with the object, it is brass plated. For normal cleaning use water, dish soap and a soft cloth or toothbrush. If the brass finish is chipped or peeling, you need to remove the top coat. In a well-ventilated area, lay down newspaper. Wearing thick gloves, apply a lacquer remover with a paintbrush or soft cloth. Polish brass with "Brasso" and buff. Use a paintbrush to apply a new coat of lacquer. Set aside to dry. Thanks for the question, Carol!

Insights into the World of Microfiber

Discover a new way of cleaning using microfiber cloths and water.

- Microfiber cloths are a fairly new textile with very fine fibers that are half the diameter of a fine silk fiber, one-third the diameter of cotton, one-quarter the diameter of wool and one hundred times finer than human hair.

- What makes microfibers so special? Many fibers are packed together to create depth and softness in the fabrics made from them. To clean with a microfiber cloth, wet the cloth and wipe whatever you want to clean; wipe again with a microfiber drying cloth or newspaper. No soap or chemicals are required and the results are amazing!

- The many microfibers in a good-quality weave are what enable the cloth to hold up to 7 times its weight in dirt, grime and liquid. When combined with tap water, microfiber cloths act like a magnet for dirt and liquid. Purchase only good-quality cloths made with 80% polyester and 20% polyamide (nylon). (Anything over 80% polyester may scratch.)

- Beware! Although microfiber cloths are now available through many retail outlets, all microfiber cloths are not created equal. Like most products on the market, you get what you pay for; look for thick, soft cloths.

- Microfiber cloths are environmentally friendly; they can reduce the consumption of cleaning chemicals in your home while cutting down exposure to toxic fumes. Microfiber cloths are especially useful for people suffering from asthma or allergies.

- Kitchen uses for microfiber cloths:
    - Shine chrome and stainless steel.
    - Commercial grade microfiber cloths remove grease, clean boil-over spills and wipe off fingerprints.
    - Use microfiber cloths to clean Corian and granite, as well as wood cabinets and the interior of microwave ovens, without soap.
    - Microfiber mops are great for both wet and dry mopping. Use the mops on kitchen floors, tile floors, hardwood floors, and to dust ceilings.

Note: Microfiber clothes are non-abrasive and will not clean up spills that require an abrasive treatment.

- **Bathroom uses for microfiber cloths**:
  - ◆ Say so long to harsh chemicals for cleaning mirrors (including hair-spray residue) and hello to microfiber cloths. Wet cloth, wipe mirror in a circular motion and dry with a microfiber drying cloth or newspaper, the mirrors will be streak free! Remember to avoid cleaning mirrors on a sunny day.
  - ◆ Clean sinks, showers and cabinets with a microfiber cloth and water.

- Uses for microfiber cloths with electronics – remove dust, dirt and finger-prints from CDs, computer and television screens with a damp wipe.

- Automotive uses for microfiber clothes – clean car glass, interior wood and plastic, leather and vinyl. Use different size cloths for different jobs – removing dirt, grime and bugs on windows.

- **Pet Uses**: Spruce up muddy paws; remove pet hair from furniture, clean up paw prints and groom pets by wiping with a damp cloth.

- Take good care of microfiber cloths. Do not wash cloths with fabric softener. Do not put fabric softener sheets in the dryer with microfiber cloths, doing so will reduce their absorbency. Microfiber cloths are heat sensitive because the fibers are extremely fine – **do not iron** (heat penetrates quickly and can scorch them).

- **Miscellaneous Uses**: Polish jewelry, patio furniture, silverware, crystal, office chairs, patio doors, boats or motorcycles. **Note**: Dry hair faster with a microfiber hair towel, they absorb wetness and reduce tangles.

- Microfiber cloths are not stain fighters, use an alternative method to zap a spot. However, a good-quality cloth will absorb 20-30% more liquid than a regular cotton cloth and shine in any finish with water.

- Microfiber furniture is gaining popularity, especially for families with small children! Although some do not like the look of this furniture, others love it. When purchasing microfiber furniture, check to make sure it is pre-treated for stain resistance to make cleaning up spills easy. It is available in formal as well as non-formal designs.

- Also gaining in popularity is microfiber in garments, especially those requiring wind resistance and water repellency. Microfiber tends to be "less clammy" in warm weather than conventional synthetics. Garments made with microfiber are usually labeled 100% polyester microfiber and often simulate the appearance of sand-washed silk. Always follow the care instructions on the label.

Brush Up on Tips that Make Sense

- Use a soft toothbrush to clean the inside window corners. **Tip**: To keep the windowsill corners free of dust and moisture, rub corners with a candle.

- Toothbrushes should be replaced every 3 months or as soon as the bristles loose their shape. Frayed toothbrushes do not clean efficiently and they can wear away the teeth and injure gums.

- Don't store toothbrushes in an open area near a toilet. The invisible spray from a flushing toilet spreads unwanted germs. Also, place toothbrushes in a dry area as wet moist toothbrushes can breed bacteria.

- Once a week toss your toothbrushes into the dishwasher in the silverware rack. Run them through with dishes to eliminate bacteria.

- Make a nifty fingernail brush by cutting down the bristles of a toothbrush.

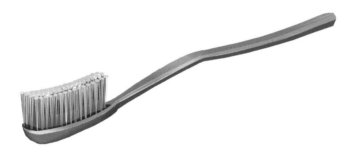

- Use an old toothbrush to clean carved furniture or picture frames. Spray furniture polish on the bristles and clean crevices easily.

- Use a camel's hair brush to remove dust or particles inside a camera.

- If your grill brush is dirty don't use it to clean your barbecue. Instead, take a ball of aluminum foil and scrub the warm grill rack, using it as you would a brush. Be careful not to burn your fingers.

- If you use a wire brush to clean your grill, wipe the grill with a cloth or paper towel before using it. Also, inspect the underside of the grill to make sure that no strands of wire are stuck on – they are dangerous if they catch in grilled food. **Tip**: You can also use a paint scraper to clean the grill.

Ways to Save Money

You work hard for your money, why throw it away?

- Feel like you're getting gray hair from choosing a wrinkle cream? Select products from a reputable company that don't recommend buying the whole product line (often many of the products aren't needed). Buy moisturizer as opposed to serum (which is generally only used in trouble areas). Choose a moisturizer with an SPF of no less than 30. Ingredient lists should contain one or more of the following: Retinoids, anti-oxidants and alpha hydroxyl acids. Retin A has proven to reduce fine lines and wrinkles. Glycolic Acid will trigger new formation of collagen  to plump cells and reduce wrinkles on the skin surface. **Tip**: Fighting acne? Proactive is an extremely effective product that will succeed where others have failed. **Tip**: Put moisturizer on over damp skin, this helps lock in moisture.

- Liquid dish detergent is available in dozens of varieties, smells, colors and brands. Choose a detergent that is gentle on hands, environmentally friendly and has a nice scent. Keep track of how much detergent is actually required to get dishes clean.

- Selecting wine can be intimidating, especially when price is an issue. For white wines: try Pinot Blanc or Sauvignon Blanc instead of the popular Chardonnay. For red wine: choose Pinot Noir instead of Cabernet Sauvignon. Look for wines produced in lesser-known regions. Try the tasting sessions at your local liquor outlet to find your favorites.

- Feed your hound the best dog food in terms of nutrients. You may bark at the price but shop around. Look for ingredient labels that list the meats first, not meal, corn or by-products (which can be animal parts not fit for human consumption).

- Never buy a shampoo based on its fragrance, this is only one ingredient manufacturers use to convince you to buy a specific shampoo. More expensive shampoos contain more surfactants, (products added to cleanse hair and create lather). Salons often sell shampoo with the following ingredients: sodium cocoyl isethionate, methyl cocoyl taurate (also labeled as coconut oil or fatty acids), cocamidoproply betaine and cocamido-propylamine oxide. These are non-drying ingredients that are gentle on hair. The quality of the surfactants determines the quality of the shampoo. Inexpensive sham-poos often contain ingredients that are harsher, e.g., sodium lauryl sulphate and ammonium lauryl sulfate. Some manufacturers mix ingredients to reduce costs by combining sodium lauryl sulphate with a coconut oil surfactant, this is an acceptable compromise.

- Save on milk by combining water and powdered milk in an empty milk jug. Your family may not notice the difference and, if it is an issue, use powdered milk only when cooking and baking. Remember, the higher the milk-fat content, the more expensive the milk.

- Avoid using soap instead of shaving cream when shaving as soap is more drying. Use shaving cream that contains a moisturizer. Also, select a shav-ing cream designed for sensitive skin even if this is not a concern, it will reduce the amount of chemicals your face absorbs on a daily basis. Foaming and scents are of little importance and are temporary benefits.

- What is the difference between deodorant and antiperspirant? Deodorant masks body odor by adding fragrances while antiperspirant reduces the amount of perspiration produced. Look for natural substitutions that con-tain no aluminum or propylene glycol. **Tip**: Apparently the Gillette Series antiperspirant and deodorant, Clear Gel, does not contain aluminum.

Edible Cleaners

- **Salt**: To clean an oven mess, sprinkle salt or baking soda on the spill. If the spill is completely dry, wet the area before applying the salt. When the oven cools, scrape away the spill and wash the oven as usual. **Tip**: Work salt into grease stains before washing to remove the spot.

- **Lemons and Oranges**: Wipe lemon juice mixed with vinegar (or baking soda) on bathroom fixtures to dissolve soap scum and hard water. This also works on dishes, surfaces and stains. **Tip**: Put lemon and orange peels through the garbage disposal to freshen the kitchen drain.

- **Banana**: Use the inside of a peel banana to polish your shoes!

- **Food Color**: Create your own colorful glue for kids' craft projects by adding a few drops of color to white glue. Or add food coloring to shaving cream and allow children to paint the bathtub walls with the colored foam. Kids will have fun and clean the walls at the same time.

- **Club Soda**: Shine floors, remove stains and clean wax build-up on vinyl by pouring a small amount of club soda on the stain. Work in sections if the stain is large. Work the solution into the surface and wipe clean. **Tip**: Club soda also works well for cleaning windows.

- **Worcestershire Sauce** and **Ketchup**: Both products are handy and effective when it comes to polishing silver, brass and copper. Pour onto a soft cloth and polish. Or polish silver jewelry by dropping it in ketchup and polishing with a toothbrush. Let stand for 10 minutes. Rinse under hot water. **Tip**: Use a pipe cleaner dipped in silver polish to remove tarnish between silver fork tines.

- **Milk**: Cowabunga! The active enzymes in milk make it a moo-rvelous cleaning agent for tackling ballpoint ink, red juices and newsprint stains. Soak the fabric in milk for a few hours and rinse with cold water before washing.

- **Cornmeal**: Absorb fresh grease stains on fabric by sprinkling cornmeal onto the area. Leave for 2 hours, brush off and wash as usual.

- **Corelleabunga Recipe**: This solution works to get rid of yellow stains on Corelle dishes caused by time and use. Prepare to be amazed! In a large pot, combine 3 cups (750 mL) vinegar, 4 cups (1 L) water and 2 tbsp. (30 mL) citric acid; bring to a boil. Set 1 Corelle dish in the boiling mixture for 5 minutes (the water must cover the dish). Once dried, your dishes will look brand new!

Cleaning Tricks for Around the House

Life just got easier!

- **Tree Sap**: To clean tree sap from hands, wipe them with mayonnaise, butter or margarine and wash as normal.

- Clean **natural wicker** with a damp stiff brush dipped in salt. Blow salt off with a hairdryer. For man-made wicker, use an all-purpose recipe. Dry immediately to preserve the finish.

 Plastic Patio Furniture Cleaner: Combine 1 gallon (4 L) warm water and 3 tsp. (15 mL) dishwasher detergent crystals. Wash, let it sit for 20 minutes; rinse.

- Clean **window screens** by laying the screen against an outside wall. Rinse with a hose to remove dust. Scrub with a nylon brush and a mixture of dish detergent and water. Dry with a towel.

- Use shaving cream to clean **plastic furniture**. Spray it on and wait for 5 minutes. Scrub with an old toothbrush.

- **Dust Less**: Add a few drops of liquid fabric softener to a damp cloth, it works as an anti-static helper. While you're at it, give the television a good wipe with the same cloth.

- **Scrubbers**: Put plastic dishwashing scrubbers on the top dishwasher rack to clean them. They last 3 times longer if you take good care of them. **Tip**: When reusing dishcloths, toss them in a dishwasher (away from heating coil) to kill any bacteria.

- **Sticky Jars**: If you suffer from unopened jar disease, wear latex dishwashing gloves when opening jars, they will give you a new grip on life.

- Cut a piece of vinyl flooring and place it under the sink to keep the cupboard floor from becoming dirty and sticky. Sponge, scrub and smile.

- **Dirty Lampshades**: Vacuum the shades inside and out. Place washable shades in a bubble bath and wipe with a soft cloth. Rinse. Remove any accessories that are not washable.

- **Thermos Dirt**: Thermos bottoms are easy to clean; attach a cloth to a wooden spoon and wipe out the thermos (also works for baby bottles).

- **Coffee Pot Stains**: Sprinkle the pot with baking soda and add a small amount of water. Heat the pot until the burnt coffee disappears (being careful not to re-burn the pot). Rinse with hot water.

- **Mini-Blind Madness**: Drop them into the bathtub and spray with the shower hose. Sprinkle with shampoo or liquid dishwashing detergent and rinse. Shake, hang to dry and move on with your day.

- **Plastic Perfection**: Clear plastic items such as wristwatches and clock faces and windshields deserve a cleaning. Apply Brasso to a soft cloth and wipe the items carefully.

- To clean baked-on ashes or soot from **fireplace glass doors**, use a damp cloth dipped in the ashes. Wipe the doors and rinse.

Oven Cleaner: Half fill a plastic container with ammonia and leave it in a cold oven overnight. The fumes will soften the baked on food. In the morning use soap, water and a scouring pad to clean up.

- Erase pencil, crayon or ink marks from upholstery using baking soda. Remove the marks with a soft brush.

- Use empty tin tennis ball tubes or a tubed potato chip can to clean a paint roller. Fill the tube with solvent to cover the roller. Close the tin tightly and shake. Let sit for 2 hours. Wash with soap and water.

- Clean golf clubs by rubbing with baby oil.

- To clean fruit stains off fingers, soaking in vinegar and rub together.

- When cleaning ivory, avoid using water; instead wipe with salt and lemon juice.

- Clean tarnished pewter by washing in hot soapy water. Polish with olive or mineral oil.

Antiqued Pewter needs a gentle touch. Combine 1 tsp. (5 mL) salt, 1 cup (250 mL) vinegar and enough flour to make a paste. Apply to pewter, let sit 10 minutes and rinse.

- To remove blue ink from the inside of a dryer use an abrasive cloth (not S.O.S, it will scratch the surface), wipe with rubbing alcohol and rinse with water.

Double-Strength TSP is useful for cleaning brick, let sit for 5 minutes and scrub. Once clean you may want to seal. Paint thinner is great at getting rid of brick stains. Wash with baking soda and water to absorb paint thinner odor. For the brick floor you can also make a scouring powder by applying 2 parts baking soda, 2 parts washing soda. Sprinkle in fireplace and spritz with water. Leave for an hour and wipe clean.

Explosive Chemical Hints (Acids vs. Bases)

- Acids and bases (also known as alkalis) are the most common types of chemical substances found in homes. Use with care.

- Acids and bases are caustic and may cause chemical burns. In chemistry, the strength of an acid or a base is measured as a pH level. A neutral solution has a pH level of 7; acids between 0-7 and bases from 7-14.

- **Acids**: Remove hard water deposits, discoloration from aluminum, brass, bronze, copper and iron rust stains; helps to produce fertilizers, metals, plastics and refining petroleum. Some acids can eat away skin, clothing, leather and metals. Examples of household acids are vinegar, citric acid, oxalic acid, hydrochloric and sulfuric acid.

- **Bases**: Soluble salts effective in removing dirt without excessive rubbing (good on grease and assisting laundry agents). Examples of household bases are baking soda, ammonia, oven cleaners, window cleaners, borax and TSP, washing soda, lye (also known as caustic soda).

- **Abrasives**: Materials that wear off dirt by rubbing with products such as rottenstone, pumice, volcanic ash, quartz, sandpaper or steel wool.

- **Detergents**: Loosen dirt; with added phosphates they are marked "heavy duty" or "all purpose" and will remove oil. Soaps are made of material found in nature. Detergents are synthetic (although some of the ingredients are natural); they are made from petroleum products and consist mainly of surfactants, foaming agents and alcohols. Since these chemicals have an unpleasant odor, detergents are usually heavily scented with artificial fragrances. Often these products are labeled as beauty, facial or cleansing bars, and sometimes even as soap.

- **Hydrochloric Acid** (also known as muriatic acid): Your stomach makes it naturally to aid in digestion. It's used industrially to process steel and in the production of batteries, photoflash bulbs and fireworks. It's even used to process sugar and make gelatin. Muriatic acid is one of the most

dangerous chemicals you can buy for home use. It is used to clean and prepare masonry for painting; removing efflorescence or mineral deposits; pH reduction in swimming pools. Use muriatic acid as a last resort, adding 1 part acid to 10 parts water, wear gloves and safety goggles and ventilate. Muriatic acid will burn through flesh. **Always add acid to water NEVER add water to acid.**

- **Phosphoric Acid**: An ingredient in soft drinks such as Coca-Cola and dental cements. Also used, as a catalyst, cleans rust off metals or porcelain, e.g., toilets. Produces phosphates, which are used in water softeners, fertilizers, and detergents. Attention has been focused on the environmentally harmful effects of phosphates in household detergents.

- **Citric Acid**: A colorless acid derived by the fermentation of carbohydrates or from lemon, lime and pineapple juices and used in flavorings and metal polishes. Citric acid is recognized as safe for use in many foods. Use citric acid on grease stains and toilet cleaning. To **remove etching** from glassware, add citric acid to the dishwasher soap dispenser or soak in ¼ cup (60 mL) citric acid and 4 cups (1 L) water for 2 hours; rinse. If etching is too far into the surface, it is permanent. Citric acid is one of the main ingredients in making bath bombs fizz. It is also the perfect solution for getting rid of soap scum on tiles. If your dishwasher, bathtub or washing machine has severe rust stains, use a chemical cleaner called "Iron Out" (while using, ventilate well and wear gloves).

Recipe for Cleaning Tile: In a bowl, add 1 cup (250 mL) citric acid to 3 cups (750 mL) cold water. Stir until dissolved. Apply to tile with a scrub brush. Rinse clean.

- **Trisodium Phosphate (TSP)**: Is available at most hardware stores in white powder form, is a cleaning agent and degreaser commonly used to prepare household surfaces for painting and removing mildew. Although it is the active ingredient in some toilet bowl cleaning tablets, TSP is generally not good for cleaning bathrooms because it can corrode metal.

- **Sodium Hypochlorite**: Is frequently used as a disinfectant and bleaching agent and normally called "bleach" (though other chemicals are sometimes given the same name). In households, bleach is used to remove laundry stains and is in many everyday cleaning products such as dishwasher soap (to break down food). **Tip**: Hot water increases the activity of bleach. A 1 in 5 dilution of household bleach with water is effective

against bacteria, and is often the disinfectant of choice in hospitals (primarily in the United States). **Warning: Never mix bleach with any substance other than water, doing so can create a poisonous gas**.

- **Acetic Acid**: Also known as ethanoic acid, is an organic chemical compound best recognized for giving vinegar its sour taste and pungent smell. White distilled vinegars are generally 4-7% acetic acid whereas cider and wine vinegars are 5-6% acetic acid. Acetic acid in the form of vinegar can play an important role in cleaning the house. Use vinegar to brighten clothes, clean countertops, deodorize, the list goes on and on.
  Tip: To remove odors, set out a rose bowl filled with vinegar, place a floating candle in the center.

- **Sulfuric Acid**: This is a strong mineral acid used for copper, steel and metal fabrication; paint, pulp, paper and fertilizer manufacturing; soap and detergent production: pigments, dyes, drugs, explosives and inorganic salts. The most natural source of sulfuric acid released into the air comes from volcanoes. Ordinary human activities also release sulfuric acid into the environment. For example, cutting onions causes a chemical from the onions to mix with eye moisture to create dilute sulfuric acid.

- **Ascorbic Acid (vitamin C)**: Is a naturally occurring vitamin found in fruits and vegetables such as citrus fruits and green peppers. Clean out hard-water stains, deodorize and sparkle the inside of the dishwasher by running a wash load using powdered lemonade mix. The ascorbic acid in the powder helps the cleaning action.

- **Malic Acid**: A colorless, crystalline compound, it occurs naturally in a wide variety of unripe fruit, including apples, cherries and tomatoes, and is used as a flavoring and in the aging of wine. **Common household uses**: malic acid can be added to skin care products to rejuvenate and improve skin conditions; also found in beverages, candy/gum, throat lozenges, mouthwash, toothpaste and soap.

- **Ammonia**: Is a compound of nitrogen and hydrogen with the formula NH_3. At standard temperature and pressure, ammonia is a gas. Ammonia has many uses in the home including removing stains and repelling moths. Use with caution, in ventilated areas and do not breath in fumes.

Caring for Pots and Pans

- Stainless steel pots and pans are a smart choice for cookware. They are moderately priced, versatile, stay shiny, do not usually dent and don't react with alkaline or acidic ingredients. However, stainless steel is not a great conductor of heat unless combined with copper or aluminum inserts, therefore, you may find that they take a while to heat up. To combat this, innovative pans have been designed with copper integrated along the sides and bottom.

- To clean copper pots and pans combine half and half salt and vinegar to remove stains. Or, scrub copper with a lemon or ketchup to remove stains. Or dip the bottom of the pot in pickle juice for 10-15 minutes; it's worth a try! If stainless steel pots are really stained, pour in ammonia, put in a garbage bag and close. Leave overnight, then wash. Or pour in pearl barley and a small amount of water, let stand overnight, then wash.

- Copper pots conduct heat evenly and quickly but are expensive and challenging to clean. Copper cools down quickly and is therefore great for sautéing. Choose copper that is lined with tin or stainless steel so that the food does not come into contact with the copper.

- Restore the shine of aluminum pots and pans by boiling apple peels in the pots for 5 minutes. Aluminum is a soft, lightweight metal that can dent easily and does react with the flavors of foods such as milk and eggs. It can be cleaned using hot soapy water. Avoid washing in hard water because it tends to darken the metal. Use cream of tartar and water to clean. Aluminum is a great conductor of heat.

- To season cast iron, rub the inside with lard, shortening or bacon grease. Heat the pan for 30 minutes at 300°F (150°C); let cool to room temperature and repeat several times to ensure proper seasoning. This creates a natural nonstick surface. Re-season as necessary over the life of the pan. **Tip**: Never store food in a cast iron pan.

- Going camping? Bring bug spray and a cast-iron pan. Although cast-iron pans are heavy, they are inexpensive and conduct heat very well. Once seasoned they do not interact with the acids in foods, and do not alter the flavors and colors; they are very durable and if taken care of can last a lifetime. Wash the hot pans quickly with hot water after seasoning, scraping as necessary. **DO NOT** use soap or scouring pads.

- Store cast-iron pots and pans between paper towels, leave lids off to prevent rust, moisture buildup and mustiness.

- If you have egg stuck on a pan or wok, pour salt over it and scrub with a paper towel dipped in oil.

- Earthenware (pottery) is made from baked clay. It conducts heat slowly and evenly, holding the heat in well. Glazes may be damaged by sudden temperature changes. Never wash with harsh scouring powders; use a mesh pad or crumpled up mesh onion bag and water to clean.

- Porcelain enamelware works well as a saucepan or roaster. Wash in hot soapy water using a nylon-scouring pad. **Tip**: Remove discoloration by making a paste of salt and vinegar. Let sit for 10 minutes and rinse.

- To figure out the number of cups that a pan will hold, use a measuring cup to fill the pan with water. Leave enough room to allow for stirring, boiling and expansion as foods get hot.

- To test a container to see if it is microwave safe. Fill a cup with water and place it in the microwave next to the dish you are testing. Run on high for 1 minute, the water should be hot, the container should not be hot. If the container is hot, it is not microwaveable.

- When buying a skillet, even if it has non-stick coating make sure it has a thick bottom. The thicker the bottom, the more control you will have over the pan. A thin pan can't handle high heat and can get hot spots or warp, making it easier for food to burn. **Note**: Throw out nonstick pans and baking sheets if the coating begins to come off. Also, cooking with lemon-based and other highly acidic foods in nonstick ware may reduce durability and the coating is more likely to peel.

- You don't need to buy a "set" of pots. Try to collect a 2-quart (2 L) saucepan, a 4-quart (4 L) saucepan, 8-quart (8 L) stockpot and a nonstick frying pan (that way you can reduce fat quantity).

- Rub a slice of raw potato on a frying pan before cooking pancakes to keep them from sticking to the surface.

- New findings suggest that non-stick cookware may not be as safe as was once believed. A report was issued that mentioned the compound – perfluorooctanoic acid (PFOA) — a "likely carcinogen" found in Teflon and other stain-resistant coatings. Research is ongoing.

Solutions 2

Solutions That Will Stick With You

- **To remove Crazy Glue**: Apply 100% acetone to the area. Also try a pumice stone for glue on fingers. For fabrics, put the item in the freezer for 10 minutes; then scrape with a plastic putty knife. Crazy Glue has an active ingredient called cyanocrylics which makes the product a super bonder.

- **Crazy Glue on wood floors:** Use fine steel wool and the solvent-based wax designed for the floor.

- **Carpet glue on tiles**: Use a heat gun, and scrape off the glue with a metal putty knife. Next, apply a paint remover and scrub the area (wear gloves). Wash with an all-purpose cleaner and leave to dry.

- Cement glue can be removed from furniture or concrete by applying cold cream, vegetable oil, peanut butter or WD-40 (test an area first).

- **Uses for double-sided tape**: Secure rugs to floors, close the edges of a pillowcase, hold fallen hems, seal envelopes and mount photos in albums.

- Stick a button to the cut end of a roll of tape, remove with each use.

- Petroleum jelly on a glue cap prevents it from sticking to the tube.

- When photographs become stuck together, put them in the freezer. To repair them allow them to separate over a 24 hour period in a basin of water. You can let them sit longer (you may have to), change the water every 24 hours. Use a pair of blunt tweezers and hold the photograph by the edges. Once the photographs have separated, rinse them. Do not let photos sit in dirty water. Photographs on plastic coated paper can be hung on a string with clothespins but **don't do this with old photos**. The old brittle paper will fall apart. Photographs can also be dried face-up on a towel.

- Apply hand lotion to your hands before working with hot glue to stop the glue from sticking to your fingers and burning your skin.

- Top of glue bottle plugged? Soak top in vinegar and poke the hole with a pin. **Tip**: If you lose the screw top for white glue, substitute a plastic cake decorator nut or a plastic wire nut for the top.

 Glue Recipe for Craft Projects: Combine 3 tbsp. (45 mL) cornstarch with 4 tbsp. (60 mL) cold water. Add 2 cups (500 mL) boiling water. Cool and use. Also, save the water from cooked rice and use as glue.

Miscellaneous Solutions

- When **skin cream** is too greasy, scoop the cream into a larger container and add a few drops of water until it becomes the consistency you desire.

- On a piece of masking tape record the name and number of the **paint color** after you paint a room. Tape it to the back of a switch plate in the room. For repainting or touch-ups, remove the switch plate, voila!

- Write your name and address on the bottom of your **trashcan** as well as on the lid for easy identification.

- Carry a package of **return-address labels** with you. It makes life easier when entering contests or leaving your address somewhere.

- Sharpen **eyeliner pencils** with greater success by putting them into the freezer for 15 minutes before attempting to sharpen.

- **To hold a poppy or corsage in place** on a shirt or sweater, cut a 1" (2.5 cm) piece of wide elastic band. Lay the elastic on the clothing and pin the flower through the elastic. Works well!

- **If you travel regularly**, keep your suitcase packed with the essentials: travel hair dryer, travel-size toiletries, hair clips, a few pieces of inexpensive jewelry, extra hairbrush and comb, travel toothbrush, shaving cream, folding umbrella and other non-perishable essentials. When you are ready to go on a trip the only items that need to be added are clothes. After returning from a trip, replenish supplies. Bon Voyage!

- When gluing lace (or any thin material) with hot glue, wear a ceramic thimble to protect your fingers.

- When sewing, tape pattern pieces to the fabric instead of pinning them. You can cut through the tape and don't have to remove pins.

- **To remove a splinter**, apply duct tape to the area. If the splinter is not too deep it should pull out easily.

- To prevent costume jewelry from **tarnishing**, store a piece of white chalk with it.

- You have a beautiful **rose centerpiece** for the table but the buds refuse to open. Lift each rose to your mouth and blow into its center to open it.

- To prevent your eyes from tearing while cutting onions, hold an unlit wooden match between your teeth. Some people have also had positive results by holding a piece of bread between their teeth.

- If you are out and about and need to measure something use paper money as your guide. The length is about 6" (15 cm) long and the width is roughly 3" (8 cm). For those who opt not to carry cash, the length of a credit card is just over 3" (8 cm).

- Rub sliding doors runners with paraffin wax to help move easily.

- Get a grip! Wear household rubber gloves to help loosen a jar lid, or place a rubber band around it for better grip.

 Extend the life of **cut flowers** by mixing a few drops of bleach and a ½ tsp. (2 mL) sugar in with the vase water.

- Hold the stems of **fresh flowers** underwater while cutting the ends off to prevent air bubbles from forming on the tips. Seal your finger over the stem end while slipping each flower into the water-filled vase.

- **Additional uses for a saltshaker**: Fill with flour and use the saltshaker to dust pans before baking. Icing sugar can also be put into a saltshaker for dusting muffins and the tops of cakes. Another idea is to put cinnamon and sugar into a saltshaker for sprinkling on toast.

- If you have washable placemats, use them as **drawer liners**.

- **"Frosted" windows for added privacy**: Combine 1 tbsp. (15 mL) Epsom Salt with 1 cup (250 mL) beer. Brush on the windows. Let dry. To remove the frost, wash off with ammonia. **Tip**: Remember to cover any wood or furniture nearby, to guard against drips.

 To clean diamond earrings**: Heat water until almost boiling; add ammonia (2 parts water to 2 parts ammonia). Put the earrings into the solution for 2 minutes. Remove earrings by holding onto the posts. Air dry. **Tip**: Never put diamond earrings in the microwave, they can burn.

- **To repair a hole in a canoe**: Drop a piece of chewed gum into the hole. Cover the area with duct tape.

- There is no need to grease a pan if you line it with waxed paper. Place pan on waxed paper and trace around the bottom; cut and lay it inside the pan.

- **Making pancakes**: Use a turkey baster when dropping batter into a frying pan. The pancakes will be nicely shaped and consistent in size.

- Inexpensive **pullover bibs for babies** can be made by cutting the sleeves and back off old sweatshirts (zig zag the edges).

Get Set for School

Are you ready?

- Medical experts agree that, as a general rule, children should not carry more than 15-20% of their body weight in their **backpacks**. The Consumer Product Safety Commission (CPSC) estimates that each year over 4,000 emergency visits to the hospital occur due to back-pack injuries. **Tip**: If the backpack forces the wearer to tilt/bend forward, it is too heavy.

- Before **choosing a backpack**, make sure that you find one with 2 padded straps and several different compartments so that the load weight is distributed evenly.

- Make school and office supply choices that are better for the environment by choosing refillable pencils and ballpoint pens. Select recycled pencils (read the label before you buy). **Tip**: Avoid toxins by purchasing non-toxic ink and crayons. If using mechanical pencils, buy spare lead and erasers. Using the supplied eraser will make refilling the pencil difficult.

- Don't throw away broken or small crayon pieces. Remove the paper from crayons and separate into colors in a muffin pan. Heat in the oven until melted. Cool and remove. Use **muffin crayons** to color pictures. If you don't have enough crayons to make separate colors, melt similar colors together or melt them all together to make 1 big muffin crayon.

- Before sending binders to school, attach a pencil with a string to the binding coils. Your child will no longer waste time searching for a pencil!

- For computer users, begin the year with a **clean screen**. Combine isopropyl alcohol and water, half and half, in a spray bottle. Spray a soft cloth and wipe the screen and key pad. Another cleaning option is CD/DVD cleaner.

- You can make your own **personalized stamp** using an eraser. Trace the eraser shape on a white paper. Draw a design inside the box and quickly push the eraser onto the paper. Apply pressure so that the ink transfers to the eraser. Using a sharp blade, cut away unwanted areas of the eraser. Ink the homemade stamp with a stamp pad. Stamp your own notepaper, books, etc. **Tip**: When writing text, create the stamp as a mirror image.

 Finger Paint Recipe: In a small saucepan, combine ½ cup (125 mL) cornstarch, 3 tbsp. (45 mL) sugar, ½ tsp. (2 mL) salt, 2 cups (500 mL) cold water. Cook over low heat for 10-15 minutes. Stir until paint mixture is smooth and thick. Remove from heat, cool and divide into muffin cups. Mix in desired food colors.

- Add dish soap to kids' paint. The soap will not affect the paint but cleanup is a breeze.

- To make your own **paint roller for kids**, remove the roll from an empty deodorant container. Fill with washable, watered-down paint. Replace roller and use. **Tip**: Use a man's shirt, put on back to front, to protect a child artist's clothing from paint spills.

- To remove price tags on school supplies, coat the area with cooking oil and scrape with a plastic putty knife.

SCHOOL TRIVIA:

The traditional quill pen was replaced by a fountain pen in 1884. The ballpoint pen became popular around 1947.

Holiday Ideas That Make Scents

Christmas Scents: To 1 quart (1 L) fir needles, add 1 cup (250 mL) dried mixed citrus peel, grapefruit, lemon, orange, lime, (coarsely broken, use blender), 1 cup (250 mL) whole rosemary, ½ cup (125 mL) dried whole basil, 2-4 bay leaves coarsely crumbled and 2 cups (500 mL) course salt (helps hold the fragrance). Mix together and use to stuff fabric tree ornaments. Hang the ornaments on your tree or add to gift packages.

- Make your own **Pomanders** (fruit studded with cloves). Choose a variety of fruits: apples, lemons, tangerines and oranges. Use a toothpick to pierce fruit skin. Insert cloves into fruit in vertical rows. Combine cinnamon, allspice and nutmeg in a zip-lock bag. Roll fruit in mixture. Shake off spice powder and wrap in tissue paper (use paper that comes in mandarin boxes). Store in a cool place for 3-4 weeks. Hang pomanders in doorways, on the Christmas tree or display in a bowl filled with potpourri.

- Consider whether or not you want to hang your pomander with a ribbon after it has dried. If so, lay a piece of masking tape the same width as your ribbon around the circumference of the fruit before you add the clove studs. Stud the rest of the fruit with cloves and then remove the masking tape.

- Before mailing out Christmas greetings, spray each card lightly with Christmas-scented air freshener.

- Although roses are not a typical Christmas fragrance, they are always popular. Make miniature dried rosebud ornaments by securing the rosebuds to a 2" (5 cm) Styrofoam ball. Fill the entire ball with roses; leave space for pinning and gluing a ribbon hanger in place.

- Stock up on the top 10 spices that remind us of Christmas: ginger, cinnamon, cloves, pepper, star anise, cardamom, peppercorns, vanilla beans, nutmeg, coriander.

- Whether you are young, old or in-between, take the time to make a gingerbread house to use as a **table centerpiece**. When company arrives place a round gingerbread cookie on each person's table setting. Use a stencil and icing sugar to monogram everyone's cookie.

- Aahhh … there is nothing like the aroma of a fresh wreath, evergreen banner or Christmas tree. When choosing fragrant branches consider: fir, pine, redwood and cedar.

- **Candlescaping** is multiple candles displayed together on a large platter. At its most complex it can be an entire room filled with candles of varying heights, sizes and shapes. Candlescaping creates a mood using texture, scent, color and light. Add greens and sparkly Christmas ornaments to the platter.

- Spicy scented candles are often inexpensive, colorful and festive. Popular holiday aromas include: chocolate (that's a given), peppermint kiss, baked apple pie, banana nut bread, cranberry crush, vanilla and sugar plum.

- **Good smell**! Combine and simmer the following yummy flavors on low heat: 3 cinnamon sticks, 3 bay leaves, ¼ cup (60 mL) whole cloves, 1 tsp. (5 mL) ground cloves, 2 tbsp. (30 mL) lemon juice, 2 pieces orange peel, ¼-½ tsp. (1-2 mL) nutmeg and 1 quart (1 L) water.

 As company enters your house, offer them a cup of **Wassail**. The aroma is relaxing, cheerful and very inviting. Combine 1 quart (1 L) apple cider, 4 cinnamon sticks, 1 whole nutmeg, ½ cup (125 mL) honey, ¼ cup (60 mL) lemon juice and 1 tsp. (5 mL) lemon peel. Simmer the Wassail on the stove or in a slow cooker and encourage guests to help themselves.

- Take a few extra minutes before company arrives to cut oranges into star shapes. Float them in punch or Wassail. **Star Shapes:** Cut oranges into horizontal ½" (1.3 cm) slices. Stick 5 cloves around slices at equal intervals. Cut out wedges between cloves.

- On the subject of **spices** keep in mind that cooking herbs and spices too long may result in bitter or too strong flavors. For soups and stews, add herbs and spices an hour or less before serving. Crush herbs before adding. Add dry spices earlier in cooking; add fresh spices and herbs toward the end of cooking.

Easy Homemade Christmas Gift Ideas

- Make your own practical and lovely **printed memo blocks**. This project will take little time and money. Simply buy a white memo block and decorate all 4 sides with paint or with stamps and a stamp pad. Tie the pad with a ribbon and a card. Perfect for an office co-worker or a teacher.

- Craft stores will have the supplies you need to create **personalized coffee mugs** using a paintbrush or cotton swab and porcelain glaze. Once decorated, bake the mugs in the oven (ask store for detailed instructions). Fill with hot chocolate mix, tea or coffee packets.

 For friends and family who love the taste of homemade cookies but don't have time to prepare them, give them **Cookie Mix in a Jar.** In a bowl, stir together 2¼ cups (550 mL) flour, ½ tsp. (2 mL) baking soda, ½ tsp. (2 mL) salt and ¾ tsp. (4 mL) cinnamon, pack into the bottom of a clean mason jar. Add 1 cup (250 mL) brown sugar followed by ¾ cup (175 mL) raisins and ¾ cup (175 mL) cup chopped nuts. Close the lid and attach a wooden spoon and a note, as follows: In a large bowl, whip ¾ cup (175 mL) butter until fluffy. Add 1 egg and ½ cup (125 mL) applesauce. Beat until well mixed. Stir in contents of the jar. Drop by teaspoonfuls onto greased cookie sheets. Bake at 350°F (180°C) for 8-12 minutes. Makes 2 dozen cookies.

- Buy blank CDs and make a **musical gift** by recording your favorite songs or holiday classics.

 Scrub-a-dub-dub, mold your own **Soap**. Here's how: Purchase a bar of color-free soap, almond oil, essential oils, e.g., lavender, rose, orange, sage, rosemary, cinnamon, etc. and food coloring. Grate the soap in a food processor. Put 5 drops of almond oil in the top of a double boiler and add the soap. Boil the water underneath and then take the boiling water and add some of it gradually to the soap mixture until it becomes the consistency of a paste. Add additional oils and color. Pour into molds, e.g., ice cube trays or spread on a pan, wait until soap is soft but holds its shape; cut with cookie cutters; air dry 24 hours. Tie bars with raffia.

 Make a **Soothing Facemask Gift**: Combine ¼ cup (60 mL) powdered clay, 3 tsp. (45 mL) cornstarch, 3 tsp. (45 mL) finely chopped herbs, e.g., peppermint, calendula and 8 drops essential oil. Add enough water to make a paste, stir and spoon into an airtight container.

Solutions 2

 Ready-to-Slice & Bake Cookies are a thoughtful gift and can be frozen until after the holidays. Combine 1½ cups (375 mL) shortening, ½ cup (125 mL) margarine, 1 cup (250 mL) sugar, 1 cup (250 mL) brown sugar, 2 eggs and 1 tsp. (5 mL) vanilla. Stir in 4 cups (1 L) flour, until soft dough forms. Divide into 6 portions; roll to form logs and freeze in pretty holiday cellophane. Add a personalized note. Cut the cookies ¼" (6 mm) thick; bake at 375°F (190°C) for 10 minutes. **Tip**: Add chocolate or butterscotch chips, chopped cherries, pecans, walnuts or coconut to the basic batter or separately.

 Make your own **Tex-Mex-Flavored Popcorn**: Combine 3 quarts (3 L) popped popcorn, 2 cups (500 mL) mini pretzels, ⅓ cup (75 mL) of EACH sunflower seeds, Cheerios and peanuts. Mix together 2 tbsp. (30 mL) grated Parmesan cheese with 1 tbsp. (15 mL) taco seasoning, ¼ cup (60 mL) olive oil and 2 tbsp. (30 mL) Worcestershire sauce. Spread onto a baking sheet. Bake at 350°F (180°C) for 15 minutes. Mix well.

 Instead of a gift basket, try making a **Chocolate Bowl Gift Holder**: Take a balloon and blow it up until the bottom half is the size that you want your bowl to be (small bowls are easier to handle). Dip and cover the bottom half of the balloon with melted chocolate. Refrigerate for 10-15 minutes. Again, dip the chocolate-covered portion of the balloon in chocolate. Refrigerate 30 minutes. Gently peel the chocolate away from the balloon. Fill with chocolate kisses. Refrigerate until giving. **Note**: If time allows, leave the balloon in the chocolate mold until it shrinks and then carefully pop the balloon.

- Make personalized recipe books, stationary, a dress-up box for kids, a decorated cookie jar or personalized photo album.

- **Refrigerator magnets** can be created using a combination of plaster of Paris mixed with water (follow instructions on the box). Decorate with acrylic paint. Glue a magnet to the back. Very affordable.

- Sew 2 small pillows using scraps of fabric. Stuff 1 with dried lavender and 1 with flax seeds to present as **eye pillows**. Let the receiver guess what they are, that should be entertaining.

- **Wine charms** are becoming popular and can be created using thin wire, a few charms from the dollar store and beads.

- Use last year's Christmas greetings to make a **placemat collage** on rectangular-shaped poster board. Cover with contact paper.

- Buy plain white **hand towels** and sew a piece of fancy Christmas lace near one end. Easy, affordable and functional, what more can you ask for?

Ways to Share a Chocolate Kiss

 Many of us now know that dark chocolate has antioxidants that help rejuvenate the skin, so why not treat yourself to a **Chocolate Facemask**? Melt 3 dark Chocolate Kisses (or 3 oz./85 g dark chocolate) in the microwave, stir in 1 tbsp. (15 mL) olive oil and 2 tbsp. (30 mL) wheat germ. Massage the warm mixture onto your face, leave for 5 minutes; rinse and dry.

- At your next party, place 1 Chocolate Kiss on each side of every name card as **place-card holders**.

- You can **make your own Chocolate Kiss** using melted chocolate and a plastic funnel. Secure a piece of greased foil in the funnel plug. Pour melted chocolate into the funnel and place in the freezer. Wait 30 minutes and release the chocolate from the mold. Wrap in foil and attach a note.

- Before bringing a friend a cup of coffee or hot chocolate, drop in 2 unwrapped Chocolate Kisses for pure luxury.

- Instead of delivering ordinary Valentine cards, create a bunch of adorable **Chocolate Mice**. Cut a 1-2" (2.5-5 cm) tall hearts from pink paper. Place it between 2 Chocolate Kisses (bottom to bottom) and secure them with glue. This is the mouse body and the heart makes the ears. Remove the top paper tags to make room for the face. Then use craft glue to attach wiggle eyes, thread whiskers and a pom-pom nose. The other paper tag is the tail. **Tip:** Make **Edible Glue**: Whisk together 4 tsp. (20 mL) All-Natural Egg Whites (Meringue Powder) and ¼ cup (60 mL) water until completely dissolved. Beat in 3 cups (750 mL) sifted powdered sugar until thick and smooth.

 For your teacher, friend, spouse, brother, sister, mom or dad, design a special Chocolate **Floral Bouquet**. Glue 2 Chocolate Kisses together (bottom to bottom). Insert a piece of 6" (15 cm) wire into 1 pointed end of the double kiss. The wire tip may need to be heated using the flame of a candle. Wrap a 4" (10 cm) square of cellophane around the Chocolate Kisses. Repeat 5 more times to make 6 Chocolate Kiss "roses." Cover the stems with floral tape and attach artificial leaves to stems. Tie all of the "roses" together with a bow. **Tip:** Colored cellophane will look even better.

- Children will love these **Valentine rockets**. Wrap red paper around a package of Life Savers. Glue a Chocolate Kiss to 1 end and a red flame made out of construction paper to the other end. On the flame write the child's name and a note that says, "You are out of this world!"

- Turn your house into a home sweet home by fashioning a Chocolate Kiss hunt throughout selected rooms. Initiate the chocolate hunt by writing clues to make the game more interesting.

 It's a simple fact; Chocolate Kisses make tasty **Instant Frosting** for cupcakes. Drop 1 kiss on top of each cupcake and heat in the oven for 5 minutes. Smooth to your heart's content.

 Recipe for **Chocolate Kiss Surprise Cookies**: Heat oven to 350°F (180°C). Remove wrappers from 1 bag of Chocolate Kisses. Mix ½ cup (125 mL) shortening and ¾ cup (175 mL) crunchy peanut butter until well blended. Add ⅓ cup (75 mL) sugar and ⅓ cup (75 mL) brown sugar. Beat until fluffy. Add 1 egg, 2 tbsp. (30 mL) milk, and 1 tsp. (5 mL) vanilla. Beat until smooth. Stir together 1½ cups (375 mL) flour, 1 tsp. (5 mL) baking soda and ½ tsp. (2 mL) salt. Add to peanut butter mixture. Shape into 1" (2.5 cm) balls. Roll in a bowl of sugar; place on ungreased cookie sheets. Bake 10-12 minutes or until lightly browned. Immediately place a Chocolate Kiss on top of each cookie, pressing down so cookie cracks around edges. Remove from cookie sheets to a wire rack. Cool. Makes 4 dozen.

- Squeeze Chocolate Kisses inside a deflated balloon. Send along a pin and a card that instructs the receiver to blow up the balloon, tie it and then pop to find the surprise.

- Fill a balloon with sweet notes and rose petals; inflate the balloon slightly and wrap as if it were a Chocolate Kiss. When the receiver unwraps the foil, the balloon will hopefully pop and the rose petals and notes will then float down.

- Using ribbon attach a group of Chocolate Kisses on the shower faucet with a note that reads. "Today you will be showered with kisses."

 Treat yourself to a soothing **Chocolate Bath**! Clean the tub with baking soda, vinegar and water. In a small pan or bowl, on the stovetop or in a microwave, heat ⅓ cup (75 mL) unsweetened soymilk and 24 Chocolate Kisses, don't boil. Fill the tub with water and add 1 cup (250 mL) bubble bath and the chocolate mixture. Enjoy!

Kitchen Secrets

Many of us have at least one shelf in our home lined with cookbooks offering intriguing recipes that look delicious yet don't always turn out the way that we had hoped. **Kitchen Secrets** is about taking those wonderful recipes and making them even better by adding the one ingredient that many of us are missing … **secrets**. This book answers questions that we have always wondered about, "How can I make fluffier mashed potatoes? Why doesn't my bread dough rise? Which flour is right for my recipe? Which is healthier, butter or margarine?" This book is packed full of answers to hundreds of questions that will enhance food and leave you smiling and your guests asking, "This is delicious, what's your secret?" You will save time and money and, more importantly, you will be proud to present your cooking!

Refer to this book before you shop, cook and bake. With every meal you will be able to take an educated bite out of life!

Common Kitchen Questions

- **WHAT IS THE BEST CEREAL CHOICE?** Good cereal choices contain "whole" grains. Protein content should be at least 3 grams per serving. Total carbohydrates to sugar ratio should be no less than 4 to 1. Zinc content should be 25-40% of recommended daily allowance (RDA). Iron content 25-40% RDA. Other vitamins and mineral content should be 25-40% RDA.

- **WHAT ARE MARSHMALLOWS?** Marshmallows were originally made using the sap from the root of the marshmallow plant? Today, marshmallows are made with cornstarch, confectioner's sugar, gelatin and water. A standard marshmallow has 20 calories and no fat. They won't dry out when frozen.

 Kitchen Secret: Don't throw away stale or soggy chips and crackers: Preheat oven to 300°F (150°C). Spread chips or crackers in a single layer on a baking sheet; bake for about 5 minutes.

- **WHAT IS VANILLA?**
  - ✦ **Pure Vanilla Extract**: To be considered pure the vanilla must be made from vanilla beans, alcohol and water and possibly sugar. Must contain at least 35% alcohol. Alcohol is the most efficient agent for extracting the flavor from the beans. Most of the alcohol burns off in cooked foods but the flavor remains intact.
  - ✦ **Imitation Vanilla**: a mixture made from synthetic substances which imitate the vanilla smell and flavor. Often contains propylene glycol, which is also found in automotive anti-freeze. Why not buy the real thing?

- **WHAT IS THE DIFFERENCE BETWEEN GARLIC SALT AND GARLIC POWDER?** Garlic salt is a mixture of garlic powder and salt, hence the name "garlic salt." Garlic powder is dehydrated garlic, which is ground into a powder. We don't need the extra salt!

- **WHAT IS PARAFFIN WAX?** This wax is often used to coat cookies with a shiny chocolate glaze. As long as it's food-grade paraffin wax, it's edible but not digestible. Which means it passes right through the body without being broken down. Paraffin is basically the same as kerosene.

- **WHAT IS SOYA LECITHIN?** It is a common constituent of animal and plant tissues, lecithin is a source of choline (a vitamin B family nutrient). It keeps oil and water from separating out, retards rancidity, reduces spattering in a frying pan and leads to fluffier cakes. An emulsifier, antioxidant in baked goods, margarine, chocolate and ice cream. Major natural sources are egg yolk and soybeans.

- ✦ Lecithin is an integral part of cell membranes and can be totally metabolized so it is virtually non-toxic to humans. One example of lecithin use is that it keeps chocolate and cocoa butter in a candy bar from separating.

- **WHAT IS YEAST?** Yeasts are single-celled fungi.
  - ✦ **Active Dry Yeast**: Yeast that has been dehydrated, just like Instant Dry Yeast to prolong the yeast storage stability. However, Active Dry Yeast differs from Instant Dry Yeast as it needs to be rehydrated in lukewarm water prior to its addition to dough. It is easy to identify each yeast. Active Dry Yeast is like tiny balls and Instant Dry Yeast is thread-like particles.

 Kitchen Secret: To test yeast for freshness, when ½ cup (125 mL) water is added to it, the volume should double.

- **WHAT IS PAPRIKA**: It is a mild to hot powdered seasoning made from sweet red peppers, high in vitamin C. Smoked paprika is fabulous.

- **BAKING SODA VS BAKING POWDER?** Both are leavening agents. Ingredients that produce a gas, which causes batters and doughs to rise.
  - ✦ **Baking soda** is sodium bicarbonate; it has no leavening capabilities by itself, but when mixed with an acid such as sour cream, molasses, lemon juice, vinegar or buttermilk gases are released. To work properly mixtures using baking soda should be baked immediately after being combined.
  - ✦ **Baking powder**: The most common type is baking soda, sodium aluminum sulfate, calcium acid phosphate and, usually, cream of tartar plus cornstarch, which is used as a drying agent. The mixture first rises when a liquid comes in contact with the baking powder. It rises a second time when the batter is exposed to heat, which is convenient because ingredients can be mixed together ahead of time.

- **WHAT IS DIM SUM?** Dim sum is not a food; it is a Cantonese term meaning, "light meal or brunch". Dim Sum is eaten morning to early afternoon with friends or family.

- **WHAT IS SOY SAUCE?** Invented in China approximately 3,000 years ago, soy sauce is made from fermented soybeans, wheat flour, water and lots of salt. If you like soy sauce, try low sodium soy sauce.

- **WHAT IS YOGURT?** Yogurt is a dairy product. The cultures in yogurt are living organisms. Yogurt is made with 2 specific live, active cultures that metabolize some of the milk sugar (lactose) in the milk into lactic acid. This action helps change the consistency of liquid milk into yogurt.

Solutions 2

- **WHAT IS THE DIFFERENCE BETWEEN DRY AND PREPARED MUSTARD?** Dry mustard is ground mustard seed and is used for seasoning vegetables, meat and in pickling. Prepared mustard is made with ground mustard seed (i.e., dry mustard), vinegar and water. The 2 types of mustards are interchangeable; 1 tbsp. (15 mL) prepared mustard equals 1 tsp. (5 mL) dry mustard.

Recipe for Mustard: In a pot combine ¼ cup (60 mL) dry mustard, ¼ cup (60 mL) white vinegar, ½ tsp. (2 mL) salt, ½ tsp. (2 mL) pepper and 1 tbsp. (15 mL) sugar. Simmer on low for 2½ hours. In a separate bowl, beat 2 egg yolks, pour into mixture and stir until thickened. Store in sterilized container in the fridge.

- **WHAT IS WHITE PEPPER AND HOW DOES IT DIFFER FROM BLACK PEPPER?** Black pepper is the dried mature berry of a woody, climbing plant called "Piper Ingram L.," which, roughly translated, means "black pepper." If the berries are intact, you have black peppercorns; if you grind them up, you get the black pepper you find on most tables. White pepper is made by soaking the ripe (but not yet dry) berries in water and peeling off their skins.

- **WHY FOOD COLORING IS USED?** People associate certain colors with certain flavors, which causes the colour of food to influence the flavor. Because of this perception, food manufacturers add dyes to many products. Have you ever tried a colorless cola? It's just not the same. The American food industry uses 3,000 tons of food color per year.

- **WHAT IS THE DIFFERENCE BETWEEN GREEN, RED, ORANGE AND YELLOW PEPPERS?** Green peppers are harvested before they are fully ripe, which is why they are less expensive than other peppers. Green peppers turn yellow and then red. Red bell peppers contain 11 times more beta-carotene (and more vitamin C) than green peppers.

- **WHAT IS THE HISTORY BEHIND WORCESTERSHIRE SAUCE?** It was created by accident in Worcester, England in 1835. When Lord Marcus Sandy returned to England from Bengal, India he asked some drug store owners to try to reproduce a favorite Indian sauce. The fish and vegetable mixture had such a strong odor that the chemists stored it in the cellar, where they forgot it for 2 years. When rediscovered, it had aged into a flavorful sauce, which was bottled and sold.

Salads

- Fruits and vegetables? Yes, mom was right, there are great benefits to eating fruits and vegetables. Pick fresh or frozen whenever possible. Avoid fruits packed in syrup; opt for those packed in water or juice. Unlike most vegetables, cooked, canned or processed tomatoes have more health benefits than fresh. **Note:** Most canned vegetables have a high salt content. Look for lower sodium options.

- Iceberg lettuce is mainly water, with practically no nutritional value. Use leaf lettuce, romaine or Boston lettuce (leaf lettuce has the highest vitamin content.) Romaine lettuce has 3 times as much vitamin C and vitamin A as iceberg lettuce. Add a little spinach, too and make your salad taste good and highly nutritional.

- Consider the following "greens" variations: **Arugula** has a distinctive peppery bite and is very popular. **Sylvetta**, another name for wild arugula, is full of flavor. Arugula makes a nice garnish for grilled steak, because it adds a lot of flavor. **Mizuna**, is a Japanese mustard green with a mild flavor. These greens are often added to **mesclun** (mixed baby lettuces and wild greens) or used alone.

- Store unwashed salad greens in the crisper section of your refrigerator, using a plastic bag with holes poked in it. Avoid storing greens next to fruits such as bananas and apples. They emit ethylene gas as they ripen. This can cause brown spots on greens and shorten storage time. **Tip:** Storing lettuce in Tupperware adds several days of freshness.

- Don't be fooled by the words, "fresh", "organic" or "natural" they don't mean clean, so be sure to wash your lettuce, fruits and veggies. Prepackaged (pre-washed) lettuce does contain a certain amount of harmless bacteria, as does all food that comes from the ground.

- When making a dressing, let the acid (vinegar, lemon juice) absorb the seasonings (garlic, shallot, spices, herbs) for at least 15 minutes before adding oil, this will bring out tasty flavors.

- The best way to check seasoning before serving a salad (which you should always do) is dip a leaf of lettuce into the dressing, this is more accurate then sampling with a spoon.

- If lettuce leaves are not dried properly, dressing will slide off damp salad greens and collect in the bottom of the salad bowl. Ensure dynamic flavor

with less dressing in your salad by washing and drying thoroughly; set leaves on a paper towel after washing.

- Garnish meals by serving pasta, sandwiches, deviled eggs or main dishes on a bed of lettuce, sliced avocado or sliced melon.

 Kitchen Secret: A nice variation is to serve hot meat/chicken straight from the grill, on top of cold crisp greens.

- Never toss your salad on salad plates. Use a large bowl that gives you room to toss; any excess oil and vinegar will be left behind in the bowl instead of in a puddle on the plate.

- Toss salad with clean hands. This will ensure that nothing is damaged and gives you more control.

 The best **Croûtons** are homemade. Melt butter, ¼-½ tsp. (1-2 mL) garlic powder and a dash of salt. Spread on fresh or stale bread. Cut into cubes and bake at 325°F (160°C) for 30 minutes.

 Potato Salad Dressing: Combine ½ cup (125 mL) mayonnaise, ¾ cup (175 mL) sour cream, 2 tbsp. (30 mL) prepared mustard, 1½ tbsp. (22 mL) ketchup, 1 tbsp. (15 mL) Worcestershire sauce, ½ cup (125 mL) diced onion and ½ tsp. (2 mL) salt and a dash of pepper. Add to potatoes.

 Kitchen Secret: Add extra color, nutrition and texture to potato salads by leaving skins on potatoes. Scrub potatoes thoroughly before cooking; 'gritty' is a texture that nobody likes in food.

- To turn a vegetable or pasta salad into a main dish, add seafood, meat, chicken or beans. To potato salad add chopped sweet pickles, red or green peppers, cucumbers, hard-cooked eggs, cheese, dill or parsley.

- Fruit salad is a colorful collection of cut fruit, berries and grapes, but there are many ways to dress it as well. One delicious dressing is to mix a few tablespoons of fresh lime juice with chopped fresh mint leaves and the juices that collect from the cut fruit

- Keep cut fruit in separate containers in the fridge until ready to make fruit salad. The fruit will stay fresh longer and the colors will not bleed.

- For a more evenly dressed salad, pour vinaigrette/salad dressing down the side of the bowl and not directly on the greens.

Secrets to Wonderful Stock, Broth & Bouillon

- The terms stock, broth and bouillon all describe the liquid remaining after cooking vegetables, meats, poultry or seafood in a flavored water. The solids are strained out and discarded and the stock is used as a base for soups. Broth is used interchangeably with bouillon, which comes from the French word, *bouillir*, to boil.

- Use only clean, cold filtered water to bring out the flavor of vegetables (beginning with hot water seals out the flavor). Broth should be brought to a boil and then simmered in order to avoid a cloudy end result.

- Fresh vegetables produce the best broth. Chicken feet add flavor to stock.

- Add dried herbs at the beginning of the cooking process. For a bold flavor add fresh herbs during the last 15 minutes of cooking.

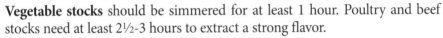

Vegetable stocks should be simmered for at least 1 hour. Poultry and beef stocks need at least 2½-3 hours to extract a strong flavor.

- Vegetable pieces such as tomato ends, carrot peels, mushroom stems, scallions, ginger peels, leeks and fennel are great choices. Add 1 or more peeled diced potatoes for added body. Turnips, rutabagas, a small amount of lentils and both fresh and dried mushroom stems, especially the trimmings from shiitakes, are all excellent choices for **vegetarian stocks**.

- Broccoli, cabbage, turnips, rutabagas, beets, asparagus, cauliflower, eggplant, parsnips and entire heads of old garlic should be left out in most cases so not to overpower the soup. There are exceptions; asparagus is essential for asparagus soup and so on.

- Once cooked, strain the liquid through a colander or, for a very clear stock, through cheesecloth or a coffee filter. Press out all the flavored liquid with a ladle or the back of a spoon. Season strained broth with salt and pepper.

- For **poultry and beef stocks**, cover the bones with cold water and bring to a simmer. After foamy suds appear on the surface (this is called a raft), skim and simmer at least 30 minutes before adding the vegetables.

- There are **2 basic ways to make chicken stock**. One method simmers a chicken carcass and vegetables and takes several hours of slow cooking. The second method uses chicken backs and wings, braising them first. It takes about 1 hour to prepare and yields a rich, delicious stock.

- If stock boils hard for any length of time, the coagulated protein and fat (scum) will be churned back into the stock which creates a greasy, cloudy stock.

- One option in freezing stock is to fill ice cube trays. Frozen stock cubes can be taken out of the trays and put into plastic bags for later use.

Making Sensational Soups

- Thin soup can be thickened: Add cream to thicken; remove vegetables from the pot, purée and return them to the pot; combine a few spoonfuls of flour or cornstarch with twice the amount of cooled stock. Return to pot.
- When soup is salty add a whole, peeled raw potato to the soup and simmer for 10-15 minutes. The potato will absorb the salt. Remove the potato or mash into soup.

 Kitchen Secrets: When reducing or boiling down a soup stock, do not add salt until the end. Whenever possible, serve cold soups on cold dishes. Serve hot soups in preheated bowls. Cold soups dull the taste buds and usually need more seasonings than hot soup. Taste and adjust before serving.

- **Bisque**: A rich, creamy soup originating from France and made from fish, shellfish, puréed vegetables or chicken.
- **Bouillabaisse**: A celebrated seafood stew from Provence made with an assortment of fish and shellfish, onions, tomatoes, white wine, olive oil, garlic, saffron and herbs. The stew is ladled over thick slices of French bread. **Tip**: Boil the broth furiously so that the olive oil will emulsify with the broth.
- **Chowder**: A thick soup containing fish or shellfish, especially clams, or corn and other vegetables.

 Kitchen Secret: When making clam chowder in the microwave, add clams just before serving and only for 1 or 2 minutes.

- **Consommé**: Consommé is a clear strongly flavored broth made from a stock, most commonly beef, veal, or poultry or fish. It makes a light and elegant start to a dinner party and is used as the basis of many classic special-occasion soups such as Madrilène (flavored with celery and tomato) and Longchamps (which has fine noodles, chervil and strips of sorrel added). For an extra-clear consommé, the straining may be done twice.

 Kitchen Secret: If you let the soup boil after it's puréed, the vegetables will become too soft and the sour cream will curdle.

- **What is roux**? Used to thicken sauces and soups, a roux is made by melting butter, adding flour and cooking it for several minutes. Liquid is then added to the roux to make a sauce.
- **Gazpacho**: This uncooked cold soup is usually made from a puréed mixture of fresh tomatoes, sweet bell peppers, onions, celery, cucumber, breadcrumbs, garlic, olive oil, vinegar and sometimes lemon juice. **Vichyssoise** is another popular cold savory soup.

- **Gumbo**: Is a roux-based soup or stew with many variations. Base is onions, celery, green pepper, garlic, roux, stock (depends on what meat you are using). Next add meat (duck, chicken, sausage, turkey) or a variety of seafood (shrimp, crab, crawfish) and vegetables. Okra is often used, but may be omitted.

- **Minestrone**: An Italian soup made with fresh seasonal vegetables, often with the addition of pasta or rice. Common ingredients include beans, onions, celery, carrots, stock and tomatoes. Minestrone is usually made out of whatever vegetables are in season. It can be vegetarian or may contain meat.

- **Stew**: A dish containing meat, vegetables and a thick soup-like broth made from a combination of the stewing liquid and the natural juices of the food being stewed. Don't lessen cooking time; simmering over low heat helps extract the maximum flavor from ingredients.

- **Mulligatawny stew or soup:** Of Indian origin, it may include cream, peppers, lamb, coconut milk, vegetables and curry. Recipes for mulligatawny were brought back to England, where it remains a popular dish, though it has undergone many changes. The name mulligatawny means pepper water or pepper soup.

- Garnish hot soups with almonds, julienned carrots, a sprig of Italian parsley, cheese, tortilla chips, bread or croûtons.

- Garnish cold fruit soups with whole berries or sliced fruit and a dollop of crème fraiche or sour cream.

- To heat or reheat soup, use a double boiler with plenty of water in the bottom. You will not burn the soup and you don't need to stir continuously.

 Chef's Secret: To remove fat from soups, drop in 2-3 ice cubes, the fat sticks to the ice cubes and is easy to scoop out.

- **Cooking with Tomatoes**: Four factors affect the acidity of tomatoes: juice, peel, seeds and overcooking. Whenever you cook with tomatoes, removing the skin and seeds will make the sauce or soup less acidic. Also, roasting onions, garlic and tomatoes instead of sautéing will reduce acids. For tomato-based soups and stews, adding mushrooms, grated carrots, a touch of sugar, a pinch of salt, a little water, milk, half and half cream or baking soda will reduce the acidity (a pinch of baking soda is all you need to lower the pH). Whatever you choose, add a little at a time until the desired flavor is reached.

Vegetable Kitchen Secrets

ARTICHOKES

- **Choose**: Artichokes with soft green color and tightly packed leaves.
- **Storage**: Do not wash before storing. Drizzle with water, place in a plastic bag, seal airtight and refrigerate.
- **Preparation**: Wash; pull off outer petals. Cut stems to 1" (2.5 cm) or less. Snip off petals tips; place in acidified water to preserve color.
- **Cooking: Boiling** – stand artichokes in large pan with 3 quarts (3 L) boiling, salted water. Optional, add olive or vegetable oil, lemon juice and seasonings. Cover and boil gently 20-40 minutes, until petals near the center pull out easily; drain. **Steaming** – place artichokes on rack over boiling water. Cover and steam 20-40 minutes, until petal near center comes out easily.
- Pull off each leaf and eat. Scrape away the fuzz in the center and use a knife to cut the heart (the best part). Serve as appetizer, salad or vegetable with seafood, beef, poultry or pork. Serve a whole steamed artichoke with melted butter and lemon.

ASPARAGUS

- A member of the lily family, which includes leeks and garlic.
- Cook 5-8 minutes in boiling water. Can be eaten cooked or raw. Peel with potato peeler.
- **Choose**: Asparagus should have a nice fragrance; closed, firm spears. Look for uniform bunches so they will all cook in the same amount of time.
- **Storage**: Snap off stem ends, wash in warm water, pat dry. Stand upright in 2" (5 cm) cold water.
- Asparagus is high in folic acid; good source of potassium, fiber, vitamins B_6, A, C and thiamine. No fat and low in sodium.

BEETS

- The fleshy root of a plant believed to have originated in North America.
- **Choose**: Firm, smooth-skinned beets with a deep red color and no spots or bruises. To ensure even cooking, choose beets that are small in size.
- Can be eaten raw, (peeled, sliced or grated), cooked (hot or cold with vinaigrette in salads and soups), canned or pickled.
- **Tip**: The leaves are delicious and can be prepared as you would spinach.
- **Storage**: Fresh beets with roots and leaves keep for 3-4 weeks in the fridge. In the basement they may become hard if left too long.
- **Cooking**: Beets hold their color better with vinegar or lemon juice added to the cooking water. Place beets in boiling water, cover; simmer until tender when poked with a fork (40 minutes-2 hours) depending on size and age of beets.
- Excellent source of potassium, vitamins A, B_6 and C, magnesium, riboflavin, iron, copper, calcium, thiamine, folic acid, zinc and niacin. Beets have the highest sugar content of any vegetable, yet they are low in calories.

BOK CHOY

- Bok choy is a traditional stir-fry vegetable from China. Only a few types of bok choy have transferred for use in the western world.
- **Storage**: Wrap bok choy in a damp towel and place in a plastic bag. Store in the crisper. Stores up to 1 week. Do not let leaves dry out.
- **Cooking**: For stir-fry, separate leaves from the thick, white stem; chop both into 2" (5 cm) wide diagonal chunks. Add stem pieces to the stir-fry first as they require longer cooking. You can also steam bok choy. Toss with a marinade.

BEANS

- Soak beans before cooking (this is vital to digestion). Add 4-5 cups (1-1.25 L) of water per cup of beans or bring water level to 3" (8 cm) above the beans. Green and red lentils and green and yellow split peas do not need to be soaked. Soaking beans avoids fermentation. Soak overnight. Drain and discard water. Rinse beans; cook OR, use canned beans.

 Kitchen Secret: Cooking beans thoroughly is one of the secrets to reducing flatulence. Another is adding ½ tbsp. (7 mL) baking soda to cooking water. Soybeans are the most difficult to digest. Legumes are easier to digest. Digestion problems are caused by sugars in the beans.

BEANS (Green and Yellow)

- Fresh green and yellow beans can be substituted for each other in recipes.
- **Storage**: Keep beans in a plastic bag in the refrigerator crisper. They will stay fresh 3-5 days. If the seeds are bulging in the pods, they are too mature.
- **Cooking**: Wash the beans, then snap or trim the cap end off each bean. Leave the beans whole for cooking or cut crosswise into 1-2" (2.5-5 cm) lengths. You can cook green beans many ways, but do not overcook or they will lose color and crispness.
- **Serving**: Top beans with any of the following: sautéed minced onion, garlic or sliced mushrooms; grated Parmesan cheese; basil, dill, lemon juice, browned almonds or peanuts; crumbled bacon, diced ham, chopped hard-cooked egg, or toss beans with salad dressing.

BROCCOLI

- **Choose**: Firm, compact clusters of small flower buds (florets). Florets should be dark green and may have a purplish cast.
- **Storage**: Refrigerate fresh broccoli in a plastic bag; use within 3 days of purchase since the vitamin content will decrease the longer it is stored. Or, stand broccoli in a jar with water to keep it fresh longer.

 Kitchen Secret: Take the rubber band off vegetables before storing; they will last twice as long.

- **Tips**: Put broccoli in cool running water just before preparing. Make fresh salads just before you're ready to eat them. Use the least amount of water and the shortest cooking time. Save the cooking water to make soup.
- **Preparation**: Trim off stalk ends. The remaining stalk is edible and nutritious. Broccoli can be blanched or boiled in a small amount of water, microwaved, steamed or stir-fried. Do not overcook so broccoli retains its bright green color, crisp tenderness and sweetness; cook just until a fork can pierce the stalk.
- **Serving**: Brush cooked broccoli with melted butter; add cheese, salad dressing or lemon juice. Cut peeled stalks into sticks, as you would carrot sticks. Add chopped, cooked broccoli to scrambled eggs and omelets, salads, stir-fries, soups, quiches and casseroles.

CABBAGE

- Cabbages range in color from pale green to purple-red with dense, compact heads with smooth, tightly packed, waxy leaves. Savoy cabbage has leaves that are brighter green and crinkled, while red cabbage has ruby red to purple colored leaves. Chinese cabbage, such as Pe-Tsai has an elongated form with tightly wrapped, pale-green leaves; Napa has yellowish-green leaves.

- **Storage**: Choose a firm, heavy head with fresh-looking, unblemished leaves; store it, refrigerated and tightly wrapped, for at few weeks. Cabbage is a very economical choice.

- **Preparation**: Wash cabbage just before using. To steam cabbage, cut it into wedges, leaving some of the center core attached to the sections to keep it from falling apart during cooking. Stew with onions and potatoes, or thinly slice it and sauté in a little olive oil, salt and black pepper. Cabbage may also be cut in fine shreds and used raw in salads or in stir-fry dishes.

CARROTS

- Bigger is not better when it comes to carrots, select carrots that are well shaped, firm, less than 8" (20 cm) long and relatively uniform in shape and size. Carrots should be a bright orange color; the deeper the color, the more beta-carotene. Nutritional values increase when carrots are cooked. Raw carrots have a tough cellular wall that is not easy to break down. Cooking carrots until they become slightly tender makes their nutrients, including beta-carotene, more easily absorbable.

- **Storage**: Before storing carrots, remove the green tops. Rinse, drain and put the carrots in plastic bags and store them in the coldest part of the refrigerator with the highest humidity. They'll last several months. To keep carrots crisp and colorful add a little bit of water in the bottom of the plastic storage bag; this will keep the carrots hydrated. Carrots should be stored away from fruits such as apples and pears. They release ethylene gas which causes carrots to become bitter.

- **Preparation**: Scrub carrots before eating. There are many glazes that can be added to cooked or stir fry carrots, try a Middle Eastern technique and top carrots with with olive oil, cumin, a little cayenne pepper and chopped herbs such as cilantro, mint and parsley.

 Chef's Secret: To make a **Carrot Flower**, wash and peel a young, tender carrot. While holding the end in 1 hand, use a sharp paring knife to make a cut toward the point to make a petal. Be careful not to cut through the end. Repeat 2 or 3 more cuts around the carrot to make the rest of the petals.

To separate the flower from the carrot, place the tip of the knife at an angle into the interior of the flower and apply slight pressure. Repeat this step for every petal until the flower breaks away from the carrot. These carrot flowers can be used singly or piled loosely together to form larger flower heads.

CAULIFLOWER

- **Storage**: Tightly wrapped in plastic in the refrigerator for up to 5 days.

 Chef's Secret: Soak a cauliflower head in ice water with the florets down to draw out hidden insects. Also, cook with florets down.

- Cauliflower is easy to prepare, but should not be over cooked. Rapid cooking and high heat are the surest ways to reduce cooking odors, maintain crispness and slow the loss of valuable nutrients. The longer cauliflower cooks, the stronger its flavor will become.

- **Preparation**: Small cauliflower heads can be cooked whole. Trim away leaves; cut out the core base. This allows for faster, even cooking. To prevent discoloration, add 1 tbsp. (15 mL) lemon juice, or 1 tsp. (5 mL) of vinegar or 1 cup (250 mL) milk to the cooking water.

 Kitchen Secret: Add a handful of celery leaves or ½ tsp. (2 mL) celery seeds to cauliflower cooking water to reduce strong odors.

- **Serving**: Sauté and top with almonds, bacon, sauce, bread crumbs, butter, cheese, chervil, chives, cream, crème fraiche, curry, garlic, ham, hollandaise sauce, lemon, mushrooms, mussels, nutmeg, nuts, olive oil, parsley, pepper, tomato sauce or walnuts

CELERY

- Look for crisp, green stalks with fresh leaves; heavy for its size.

- **Preparation**: Rinse well in cold water; separating stalks slightly. Cut off base and tips of leaves. Enjoy celery as is, or cut crosswise into short lengths for party and relish trays. Serve with dips and the traditional favorite, peanut butter or with soft cheeses, such as Blue or Gorgonzola. This is the only raw vegetable that is so much work to eat; you actually burn calories eating it.

- Celery is usually eaten raw but can also be braised or stewed, alone or with other vegetables. Celery leaves are great additions to soups and stews.

- **Storage**: Keep celery in the refrigerator crisper. It will last several days. For longer storage, stand the celery head in a jar or a container of cold water, wrap the exposed portion with a plastic bag.

CORN

- Select corn with firm, fresh husks. The tassels should be pale and silky, with only a little brown at the top. Hold the ear in your hand: if it's warm, it's starting to turn to starch; if it's still cool, it's probably fresh.
- **Storing**: Store corn in the refrigerator.
- **Preparation**: Don't add salt to the water when boiling corn, it toughens the kernels; instead, add a pinch of sugar. Fresh, sweet corn only needs a few minutes, cooking time. Bring the water to a boil before dropping in the shucked ears. If the ears are too long for the pot, don't cut them with a knife, break them in half. Let the water return to a boil and boil hard for 3-4 minutes. Remove immediately and serve; don't let the corn stand in the water.
- To **Grill Corn**; pull down the husks but don't detach them; remove the silks. Spread butter and salt on the kernels, pull the husks back up and twist closed. Grill the ears for about 15 minutes, turning often.
- Leftover corn can be added to soups, fritters, or bread.

 Kitchen Secret: A dampened paper towel or terry cloth brushed downward on a cob of corn will remove every strand of corn silk.

CUCUMBERS

- Love them with vinegar, salt and pepper; nothing says "tea party" like cucumber sandwiches.
- **Varieties**: **English cucumbers**: Have few seeds and thin skin. **Gherkins**: Tiny cucumbers with bumpy, almost warty skins; mostly pickled and eaten with cold meats. **Kirby's**: Small cucumbers, used for pickling. **Ridged cucumbers**: Have a thick, bumpy skin. Available only in specialty grocers.
- **Choosing**: Cucumbers should be firm from top to bottom.
- **Storage**: They are sold prewrapped in plastic and can be stored in the fridge crisper for up to a week. Remove the plastic packaging once you've "started" a cucumber. Discard once the cucumber begins to go soggy.
- **Preparation**: Wash cucumbers even if you don't peel them. Peel cucumbers with wax coatings. Special citrus peelers can remove strips of peel to give an attractive striped effect when sliced.
- **Serving**: Salad favorites, thinly sliced cucumbers are most frequently served with a light dressing or sour cream but are also good cooked. To cook, cut the cucumber into wedges, remove the seeds then simmer for a few minutes or until tender. Drain, return the cucumber to the pan; stir in a little cream and seasoning.

Chef's Secret: To make a **Cucumber Spiral** garnish, use a sharp knife to cut off both ends at a 45° angle. Continue slicing at an angle along the cucumber, being sure not to cut all the way through. Cuts should be ¼" (6 mm) slices. Use on salads, sandwich platters or cold soups. This cut also works with zucchini or kiwi.

LEEKS

- Related to garlic and onions, leeks have a subtle, sweet flavor. They enrich soups or stews and are delicious with potatoes and cheese.

- Buy small or medium leeks; large leeks (over 1"/2.5 cm in diameter) are likely to be tough and woody. Leaf tops should be fresh and green; the root end should be unblemished and yield very slightly to pressure. Buy more than needed to allow for losses due to trimming.

- **Storage**: Loosely wrap in plastic (to keep them from drying out and to contain their smell) they will keep in the fridge for a week.

- **Preparation**: Remove damaged outer leaves. Trim the rootlets at the base and cut off ½-⅔ of the dark green tops. Partially cut the leeks in half lengthwise, starting at the middle and running the knife up to the green tops. Make another lengthwise cut perpendicular to the first, fanning the leaves. Rinse well to remove any dirt. If chopping them, give them another wash.

- Undercooked leeks are tough and chewy; overcooked leeks can take on an undesirable texture. Cook until just tender; test by piercing the base with a knife. Braising in a moderate oven will take from 10-30 minutes depending on size. They can also be boiled or steamed.

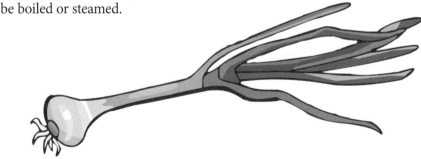

MUSHROOMS

- Mushrooms should look fresh and free from major blemishes; edges may be somewhat uneven. There are over 2,500 mushroom varieties. Fresh gourmet mushrooms offer a variety of distinct flavors and textures.

- **Shitakes** have a rich, earthy flavor and a firm, meaty texture (must be cooked). Add to stir-fries or grill and top with Parmesan cheese.

- **Oyster Mushrooms** must be cooked briefly. Combine oyster mushrooms with seafood, chicken, soup or omelets.

- **Enoki** can be served raw or lightly cooked. Add to salads and sandwiches for appealing crunch or use as a garnish for soups and main dishes.

- **Portobellos** have a meaty texture. Brush caps with oil or salad dressing to keep them moist during grilling or roasting. Use in sautés, sauces, soups and stews. Grill or broil whole and serve as "burgers" or use as pizza "crusts" with favorite toppings.

- **Storage**: Remove mushrooms from plastic, place in paper bags or cover with paper towels and refrigerate. Stored properly, specialty mushrooms will keep about a week. Shitakes will keep even longer.

- **Prepartion**: There is no need to peel mushrooms. Trim stem end if it's dry, or the tough Shiitake stem or Portabolla root. Prepare along with the caps.

- Mushrooms can be brushed, sliced thick or thin, cut in quarters, coarsely or finely chopped using a sharp knife. If a recipe calls for just caps, twist stems loose or separate them from the caps with the tip of a knife.

- Sauté, roast or grill and season. The most popular way to cook mushrooms is to heat butter or oil in a large skillet. Add mushrooms. Cook and stir until golden and any juices have evaporated, about 5 minutes. Don't overcrowd the skillet or the mushrooms will steam rather than brown.

ONIONS

- The Ancient Egyptians worshiped the onion, believing that its spherical shape and concentric rings symbolized eternity.

- Onions are one of the most important cooking ingredients to have on hand. Choose from sweet, sharp, mild, or pungent. The onion family includes chives, scallions, leeks, shallots, garlic, red onions, yellow onions and white onions. About 88% of onions used are yellow with about 7% red onions and 5% white onions.

- **Storage**: Onions should be kept in a cool, dry, open space, away from bright light, with air circulation. Do not store onions below the sink or near potatoes because potatoes produce a gas that causes onions to spoil more quickly. Spring/summer onions usually store for about 2 weeks.

- **Preparation**: Onions may be eaten raw or cooked; they may be boiled, braised, baked, microwaved or sautéed.

- The trick to chopping an onion, use a sharp knife. Cut off the stem end and then cut the onion in half lengthwise. Remove the skin and make parallel cuts across the onion – but do not cut through the onion. This helps hold the onion together and also ensures that the least amount of tear-inducing fumes are released. Finish with a series of slices and you have a perfectly chopped onion.

 Chef's Secret: **Green Onion Brush Garnish**: Cut off the root end; place the onion on a cutting board; starting about 1" (2.5 cm) from the green part of the onion, use a sharp knife and make several lengthwise cuts through the white part of the onion; make your cuts as close together as possible. Cut off the green stalk leaving about a 1" (2.5 cm) uncut section above the cut part. Place in ice water until ready to use. The cut onion will curl and flair out like a brush or broom.

PEAS

- Peas belong to the legume family.
- Select medium-sized peas that are firm, crisp, with a bright green color and a fresh appearance. Avoid tough, thick-skinned pods.
- Boil peas for 3 minutes; soak them in ice water to set their bright color and then use them in a stir-fry with other vegetables, shrimp, chicken or pork. They can also be cooked by themselves with butter and herbs. Or blanch peas for a minute in boiling water. Drain and cool promptly in cold water and they are ready to be added to salads and pasta dishes.
- There are two categories of peas: those with edible pods and those without.
- **Green, English and Garden** Peas have inedible pods.
- **Petit pois** are green peas that have been picked before full maturity so they are smaller than normal green peas.
- **Snap peas** look like miniature green peas except the pods are edible.
- **Sugar Snap** and **Sugar Daddy** are two varieties of snap peas. The Sugar Daddy is a cross between green and snow peas and is a string-less sugar snap pea. You don't have to remove strings from Sugar Snap peas.
- **Snow peas** have flat, wide, pale green, edible pods with the outlines of little peas visible throughout the pod.

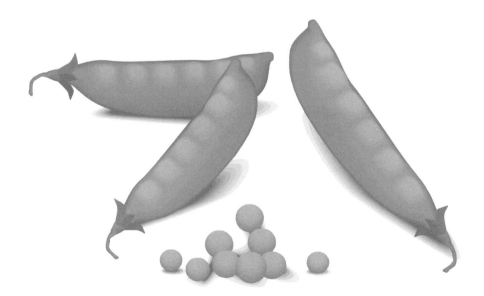

POTATOES

Some of the many varieties of potatoes are:

- **Russet (Idaho potato)**: This is the most popular potato in North America. High in starch, they are characterized by netted brown skin and white flesh. Russets are light and fluffy when cooked, ideal for baking, frying and roasting. Russets are also best for fluffy, mashed potatoes because they absorb liquid.

- **Round white**: Medium in starch and have smooth, light tan skin with white flesh, creamy texture and hold their shape well after cooking. An all-purpose potato, round whites are versatile and work well in just about every potato preparation.

- **Round red**: Have red skin and white flesh, a firm, smooth, moist texture, making them well suited for salads, roasting, boiling and steaming.

- **Storage**: Choose potatoes that are firm and free of sprouts, green skin or spots. Green potatoes may contain a substance called solanine, which is bitter and can be toxic. If potatoes have turned green, trim off the green areas before using. To prevent potatoes from greening, they should be stored in a dark, cool place that is well ventilated. Such storage will prevent potatoes from "sprouting." Potato sprouts are poisonous; cut off the sprouts and they are fine for eating. A sprout of any size is toxic, but you would have to eat many sprouts to get sick. Store an apple with potatoes to prevent sprouting. Avoid storing potatoes with onions.

- **Serving size**: Estimate 6-8 oz. (170-250 g) raw potato per person.

- Keep cut, uncooked potatoes in cold water until ready to use, for up to 2 hours. However, extended storage in cold water is not recommended as it can result in loss of some of the potatoes' water-soluble nutrients.

- Sweet potatoes are often mistakenly called yams; they are not the same.

- The potato is the fourth most important world crop, after wheat, rice and corn.

- For less watery **mashed potatoes**, peel them after boiling instead of before. This helps keep the flavor in. **Tip**: Put potatoes in water with ½ tsp. (2 mL) salt and just enough water to cover them.

- Potatoes peeled ahead of time and starting to darken should be cooked with milk. Do not let the milk come to a boil, this will help lighten the potatoes.

- Test potatoes for doneness using a knife. If the potatoes cling to the knife, they are not done. If the potato slides out easily, they are done. Drain and dry potatoes for a minute on cooking element before mashing.

- Using a ricer to make mashed potatoes will remove lumps. If a ricer is not available use a waffle type masher.
- Heat and combine milk and butter before adding to mashed potatoes. **Tip**: Some people add liquid first instead of butter to make potatoes lighter others argue that butter should be added first. Add buttermilk, cream, sour cream, crème fraiche, mascarpone cheese or cook in broth to add flavor.

 For **Garlic Mashed Potatoes**: Add garlic cloves to potato water when cooking or sauté onion or garlic and add to mashed potatoes before serving.

- Sprinkle potatoes with nutmeg, chives, Parmesan cheese, bacon or roasted garlic before mashing. Season with salt, pepper, mustard or fish sauce.
- Potatoes can become sticky/gluey when mashed in a food processor.
- Mashed potatoes can be made ahead of time. Cover with plastic wrap and store in fridge for up to 6 hours. Reheat before serving.
- Leftover mashed potatoes can be fried the next day; they are delicious.

 Potato Pancakes: Using a food processor, grate 4 peeled potatoes and 1 medium shredded onion. Squeeze out excess liquid. Beat in 2 eggs. Mix in 1 tbsp. (15 mL) flour, 1 tbsp. (15 mL) melted butter or margarine, 1 tsp. (5 mL) baking powder, salt and a sprinkle of pepper. In a greased frying pan drop ½ cup (125 mL) of mixture, fry and turn to brown other side. Yields approximately 10 pancakes.

RADISHES

- Choose radishes that are firm, crisp and without blemishes. The greens should look fresh. The most common radishes are the small, round Cherry Belle, the Red Globe radish or the white carrot-shaped Daikon. The two main categories are spring and winter radishes, based on harvest time. Spring radishes have a short growing, season, resulting in a smaller radish they are generally eaten raw. Winter radishes have a longer growing season, which results in a larger round or more elongated radish that stores longer. Winter radishes are generally cooked.

- **Storage**: Store without the leafy tops and refrigerate to keep fresh for 4-7 days for spring varieties, or 2-4 weeks for winter radishes. The larger varieties are similar to turnips for storing and can be kept longer or stored in a cool dry area.

 Chef's Secret: **Radish Flowers** for garnishing. Wash radishes. Start from the root section and cut downward, along the edge of the radish almost to the bottom of the stem section, leaving the red skin intact. Make 4-6 petals. Repeat the slices inside the cuts you've already made, being careful to leave a strip of red skin intact on each petal. Do not make this row of cuts as deep as the first row. Place rosettes into a bowl of ice water and soak them for about 15 minutes to make them bloom.

SPINACH

- Spinach consumption has boomed over the past fifteen years and this is due to the popularity of plastic bags of triple-washed spinach in the supermarket in particular, baby spinach. Spinach has a sandy almost dirty feel when not completely washed. Avoid spinach that is bruised or slimy. Store spinach in the fridge up to 4 days. Fresh spinach is sandy, so rinse thoroughly before using. To clean, place spinach in a sink or basin and fill with cold water to cover. Agitate the leaves to remove the dirt. Lift the leaves from the water and set aside. Drain the sink or basin and rinse out the dirt and sand. Repeat until no grit remains.

 Kitchen Secret: To wash gritty, sandy vegetables like spinach, leeks and arugula, place the trimmed vegetables in a large bowl of lukewarm water. Add 1 tbsp. (15 mL) of kosher salt, toss and let stand 20-30 minutes. Then carefully lift the vegetables from the water and place in a colander. There will be sand at the bottom of the bowl but not much on the vegetables. Rinse in the colander.

SQUASH and PUMPKINS

- **Preparation**: Winter squash and pumpkins mature on the vine and develop an inedible, thick, hard rind and tough seeds. Because this rind makes most of them difficult to peel, it's easier to cook them unpeeled, then scoop out the cooked flesh. Wash the exterior just before using. Scoop out seeds before or after cooking.

- To cut in half, grasp the squash or pumpkin and use a sharp knife to slice through to the center. Then flip and cut the other side until they fall open. Remove and discard the seeds.

- To bake a whole winter squash, pierce the rind with a fork and bake in a 350°F (180°C) oven 45 minutes. Test for doneness by piercing with a fork.

- Boil or steam squash quarters or rings 25 minutes, or until tender.

- All varieties are great for puréeing, roasting and baking. Once squash or pumpkin is cooked and mashed, it can be used in soups, main dishes, vegetable side dishes, breads, muffins, custards and pies.

- Boil or mash as you would potatoes. Or add peeled cubes to soups, stews, beans, gratins and vegetable ragoûts.

- Dress any cooked winter squash with butter and herbs, a cream sauce, cheese sauce, maple syrup and nuts, marinara sauce or stewed fruit.

TOMATOES

- Tomatoes are botanically classified as fruit. After buying tomatoes, they should be left at room temperature until they are ripe. The ideal temperature for tomatoes is 55°F (13°C). If stored at lower temperature, the flavor and texture of the tomato will be affected. Tomatoes used for eating raw should not be stored in the refrigerator. If the tomatoes will be used for cooking, ripened tomatoes may be stored in the refrigerator for about 10 days. For long-term storage, chop ripe tomatoes, seal in zip-lock freezer bags; freeze.

 Kitchen Secret: Sunlight doesn't ripen tomatoes, warmth does. Store tomatoes with stems pointed down and they will stay fresher, longer.

 Chef's Secret: Tomato Roses: Cut a base from the stem end of each tomato, but do not sever. Cut a continuous narrow strip in a spiral fashion, tapering end to remove. Curl strip into its base in a rose shape.

TURNIPS/RUTABAGAS

- Turnips (white with a purple top) and rutabagas (yellow turnip – thought to be a turnip/cabbage cross) are both members of the cabbage family.
- **Storage**: Buy the smallest, youngest turnips available. They should be firm, smooth and unblemished, ideally with fresh green tops. Store in a cool dry place.
- **Preparation**: Young turnips should not need peeling, trim and simmer or steam until tender. They are delicious raw, thinly sliced or grated into salads. Peel older turnips and then slice or dice before cooking. Older specimens smell strongly if overcooked. To avoid this, blanch turnips if they are to be served as a vegetable dish, or add sparingly to soups and casseroles, so that the odor is dispersed.

ZUCCHINI

- **Preparation**: Peel and slice zucchini down the middle lengthwise and fill with ground beef, top with spaghetti sauce and cheese and bake, or add grated zucchini to soups and salads, eat raw or bake comfort food, e.g., zucchini cake and cookies.
- **Storage**: Because of its versatility, zucchini is a good staple. Choose young tender zucchini. Wash and grate. Steam; blanch in small quantities, 1-2 minutes, e.g., until translucent. Pack in measured amounts into containers, leaving ½" (1.3 cm) headspace. Cool by placing the containers in cold water. Seal and freeze. If watery when thawed, discard the liquid before using the zucchini.

 Kitchen Secrets:

- ✦ Cook green vegetables for 7 minutes or less so they keep their green color and look appetizing. After cooking, submerse them in ice water to lock in the vibrant green color.
- ✦ Perk up wilted vegetables by soaking in 2 cups (500 mL) water and 1 tbsp. (15 mL) vinegar.
- ✦ Don't throw away overcooked vegetables, purée them and add milk to make a cream soup or pour the purée over cooked meat to create a tasty and healthy gravy.
- ✦ To keep a cutting board from slipping as you chop, or a bowl from sliding as you mix, dampen a paper towel and place it under the board or bowl before you chop.

Fruit Kitchen Secrets

APPLES

- Apples are a member of the rose family. By some estimates there may be over 10,000 different apple varieties. Apples have been cultivated for centuries and new varieties have continually arisen or been developed. Refrigerate apples, they last much longer and spritz with water every few days. Remove any bad apples because one bruised apple can ruin the entire bunch. Apples are ripe when picked and high in fiber, the most popular apple in North America is Red Delicious.

HOW DID GRANNY SMITH APPLES GET THEIR NAME?

ANSWER

The tart green apples were first grown by a gray-haired grandma, Maria Ann Smith, in a suburb of Sydney, Australia.

APRICOTS

- The apricot is one of the oldest cultivated fruits. It is said to have existed in northern China 4,000 years ago. Because of its fragrance and good keeping properties apricot kernel oil is often used as a base for skin care products. Its positive effect on the moisture content of skin makes it particularly beneficial for dry, chapped and sensitive skin. It makes skin soft, firms tissues and promotes cell renewal.

- Store unripe apricots in a paper bag at room temperature away from heat and direct sunlight. Once ripe, usually 2-4 days, apricots will keep for a day or two, if stored in a plastic bag in the refrigerator. Let them come to room temperature before eating and don't wash them until you are ready to use.

BANANAS

- Avoid bruised bananas and bananas showing splits in the skin. Choose firm, green to slightly yellow bunches and store them at room temperature. It is claimed that bananas taste sweeter ripened off the plant. Eat or prepare bananas when they ripen to a uniform yellow with tiny brown flecks. The skin of bananas turns black when they are refrigerated, though it does not affect the quality of the fruit inside. Very ripe fruit can be peeled, frozen in freezer bags and used for baking. As bananas ripen, the starch in the fruit turns to sugar. Therefore, the riper the banana the sweeter it will taste. Do not throw away overripe bananas; they are the best for making moist banana loaf and muffins.

 Kitchen Secret: Like apples, stored bananas give off ethylene gas, which causes fruit to ripen quickly. Hang bananas so that the air can flow through them and they won't ripen as quickly.

FRUIT TRIVIA:

Three medium-sized bananas weigh approximately 1 pound (500 g).

A cluster of bananas is called a hand and consists of 10-20 bananas, which are known as fingers.

BLUEBERRIES

- Did you know that early American colonists made gray paint by boiling blueberries in milk?

- Blueberries must be ripe when purchased as they do not continue to ripen after harvesting. Avoid soft, watery or moldy blueberries. Stained or leaking containers are an indication of fruit past its prime. Keep blueberries refrigerated, unwashed, in a rigid container covered with clear wrap. They should last up to 2 weeks if they are freshly picked. Water on fresh blueberries causes them to deteriorate; do not wash before refrigerating and avoid those at your grocer's that are exposed to mist sprayers used to keep greens fresh.

CHERRIES

- Fresh cherries should still have their stems attached and be clean and dry. Avoid cherries that are hard, small, and/or lighter in color because they were probably picked before they were ripe. Also avoid soft or sticky fruit with a dull cast and shriveled skin since they are probably overripe.

• It is very important to store cherries in the coldest part of the refrigerator.

KIWI

• This fruit is named after the "kiwi" birds native to New Zealand. Choose semifirm, unblemished fruit with uniform skin. Kiwis sweeten with age but should be consumed before they become mushy; they will ferment if left too long. Refrigerate when soft. To eat, scoop it out with a spoon or peel and slice.

LEMONS/LIMES

• When choosing lemons and limes look for a smooth skins with a little give; they should feel heavy for their size. Large fruit are best for zest. Store them unbagged in the fridge, but let them sit at room temperature for a few hours before using. If you use them often, store on a counter. They last 10 days to 3 weeks refrigerated; up to 1 week at room temperature. To get more juice, roll lemons and limes between hands before squeezing.

MANGOS

• The mango is known as the 'king of fruit' throughout the world. A ripe mango has a full, fruity aroma. The best-flavored mango has a yellow tinge when ripe, however, color may be red, yellow, green, orange or any combination. Mangos have a shelf life of 1-2 weeks. The best way to ripen a mango is at room temperature, on the kitchen counter and if you wish to quicken the process place in a paper bag overnight.

ORANGES

• Oranges are the most important citrus crop in the world. Select oranges with a shiny skin free of blemishes, wrinkles, soft areas, or mold. They should be heavy for their size indicating they are full of juice. (Most citrus is waxed to replace natural wax that is removed during the washing process.) Lighter fruit has more skin and drier pulp resulting in less juice. Select navel oranges with small-sized navels, oranges with larger navels indicate they were over-ripe when picked. Store oranges in a cool place outside the refrigerator and try to eat them within a few days. To keep them longer, refrigerate in a plastic bag or in the vegetable crisper.

PEACHES

- The red blush on peaches may not always be a true sign of maturity. Choose peaches with a yellow or creamy background, fragrant, unblemished and not too hard. Wash peaches before using. Peaches will peel more easily if blanched for a minute in boiling water, then plunged into cold water for a minute to cool. Use peaches in fruit or pasta salads or grill peach halves and top with blueberries and brown sugar for dessert. Blend into frozen daiquiris, smoothies or shakes. Top with frozen yogurt or angel food cake.

 Kitchen Secret: Peaches should be sprinkled with lemon or lime juice after cutting to prevent discoloration. To ripen peaches, store in a brown bag at room temperature. Store ripe peaches in the crisper for up to 5 days.

PEARS

- To hurry the ripening process, keep pears at room temperature, each pear individually wrapped in paper, or enclosed in a paper bag ventilated with a few holes. Pears seem to ripen from the inside out. Looks can be deceiving, so test the stem end for a slight "give" to tell you when the pear is ready.

PINEAPPLE

- The pineapple was named because of its resemblance to the pinecone. Pineapples do not ripen after harvest and are therefore difficult to export. Avoid green pineapple, as they will not be sweet. Inspect the fruit and avoid those with soft or dark spots and mold. The ripe fruit should have a pleasant fragrance; if not, it may indicate that fermenting has begun. Another indication of ripeness is if one of the green spikes can be removed easily from the crown. Tug on a leaf from the top. If the leaf feels loose the pineapple is ripe. Fresh pineapple can be stored in the refrigerator up to 5 days. Freeze for longer storage; remove the rind and core, cut into chunks.

PLUMS

- Plums are related to cherries and peaches, choose plums that are tender to the touch and that have smooth, uniform skin. Look for those that retain the "bloom," a natural powder-like haze covering the fruit, since these are likely

to have received the least handling. When plums are picked before they are ripe, they can be ripened at room temperature, or placed in a paper bag with an unripe banana for a day or 2. In the refrigerator, ripe plums keep for about 4 days.

RASPBERRIES

- Raspberries are available in red, black and purple varieties. Fully ripe berries should be the correct color of their variety. Red raspberries should be deep red. Black and purple varieties should not have red, unripe areas. All varieties should be plump, firm and hold their shape well. Avoid soft, juicy berries and berries in stained boxes.
- Raspberries are highly perishable. They must be used soon after picking or purchase. Store raspberries in the refrigerator, in a covered container, for up to 3 days. Wash the berries in cool water just before using.

RHUBARB

- If you really want to get your pots clean, cook rhubarb in dirty pots and they will shine! Although not strictly a fruit, the bright crimson stalk of this leafy perennial plant is commonly considered one. Rhubarb leaves should be discarded as they are toxic. Stalks should be crisp. Avoid stalks that are thin, limp, or battered. Rhubarb can be tightly wrapped and stored in the refrigerator for 1-2 days. For longer storage, freeze after blanching and cutting stems into chunks.

STRAWBERRIES

- There are many explanations about where the strawberry got its name. Some believe that the name came from the practice of placing straw around the growing plants for protection, others believe the name originated over 1,000 years ago because of the runners which spread outward from the plant. Choose berries that are firm, plump, free of mold and which have a shiny, deep red color and attached green caps. Since strawberries, once picked, do not ripen further, avoid those that are dull in color or have green or yellow patches since they are likely to be sour and of inferior quality. Before storing in the refrigerator, remove any strawberries that are moldy or damaged so that they will not contaminate others. Replace unwashed and unhulled berries in their original container or spread them out on a plate covered with a paper towel, then cover with plastic wrap. Strawberries will keep fresh in the refrigerator for 1-2 days. Do not leave strawberries at room temperature or exposed to sunlight for too long, as this will cause them to spoil.

- **To freeze strawberries**, first wash them gently and pat them dry. You can either remove the cap and stem or leave them intact, depending upon what you will do with them once they are thawed. Arrange them in a single layer on a flat pan or cookie sheet and place them in the freezer. Once frozen, transfer the berries to a heavy plastic bag and return them to the freezer where they will keep for up to 1 year. Adding a bit of lemon juice to the berries will help to preserve their color. While strawberries can be frozen whole, cut or crushed, they will retain a higher level of their vitamin C content if left whole.

 Kitchen Secret: When cooking any strawberry dessert, add a splash of aged Balsamic vinegar to the recipe to bring out the strawberry flavor.

 Chef's Secret: To make **Chocolate-Covered Strawberries**, push a toothpick into the strawberry stem. Dip each strawberry into melted dark chocolate, allowing any excess to drip off. Dry on waxed paper. When chocolate has set, drizzle melted white chocolate over each berry. Store in refrigerator for up to 24 hours or eat as desired.

 Chef's Secret: Garnish desserts with frosted fruit. Coat the fruit with beaten egg white, roll it in fine icing sugar, let dry overnight. Or glaze cut fruit with melted apricot or strawberry jam.

WATERMELON

- A new study shows storing watermelon in the fridge can reduce its nutritional value. Seeded watermelon chunks can be frozen to use in watermelon slushes or fruit smoothies. Watermelon rind makes a great base for a fruit basket. Select a firm, symmetrical watermelon that is free of bruises, cuts and dents. Turn the melon over. If the underside is yellow and the rind has an overall healthy sheen, the watermelon is probably ripe. Select melons that are heavy for their size. Watermelons are 92% water, which obviously accounts for most of their weight. A good rule of thumb is to buy the melon size that will satisfy your needs, so you don't waste any. Wash watermelons before cutting.

Eggstra-ordinary Tips

- The next time someone drops an egg on a hard-surfaced floor, sprinkle the egg with salt. Let stand for 5 minutes and wipe up the egg with no mess.

- Recent studies indicate that eggs are cholesterol neutral. They are an excellent source of Vitamins A, D and E. Low-cholesterol eggs are also available. Egg whites are awesome! The protein in an egg white is documented as one of the purest forms of protein. Six egg whites deliver 15 grams of protein, only a trace of carbohydrates, no fat and no cholesterol. **Note:** When whisking egg whites, add a pinch of salt for more volume and be sure that eggs sit at room temperature before whipping.

- The easiest way to tell if an egg is fresh is to immerse it in a pan of cool salted water. If the egg sinks, it is fresh; if it rises throw it away.

- Boil eggs without breakage by following a few simple steps: begin by soaking eggs in warm water prior to boiling. Add 1 tbsp. (15 mL) of vinegar to the pot. This will reduce the number of broken eggs as well as reducing foul odors. Or, poke the end of each egg with a pin to release the gases and lessen the chances of breakage, this also prevents the yolk from graying and cuts down on odor. **Tip:** If an egg cracks while cooking, wrap it in aluminum foil and continue to boil.

- Hard-boiled eggs will be easier to peel if they are submerged in cold water after cooking and peeled under cold running water.

- Always store eggs with the wide end up, this keeps the air pocket in the large end and the yolk in the center. **Note:** Remember, eggs are porous, therefore storing them in their original carton will prevent them from picking up a variety of smells from inside the fridge.

- Instead of hard-boiling eggs for decorating purposes, empty them. The shells will keep indefinitely (if they do not crack during preparation). Wash and dry an egg, using a sterilized needle, prick a hole in each end. Chip away bits of shell until it is big enough to fit the tip of a kitchen baster. Shake the egg until the inside comes out. Rinse and dry; cover the open hole with wax and decorate.

An option when **Dying Easter Eggs**: Use natural colors as opposed to commercial (the eggs will not need to be boiled ahead of time). Add ½ tbsp. (7 mL) of vinegar plus the dye (listed on page 138) to a pot of cold water before cooking the raw eggs. Bring the eggs to a boil, reduce heat and let simmer 15 minutes.

Homemade Colors include: brown – onion skins, tea or coffee. Yellow – turmeric or saffron. Red – cranberries. Purple – beets or purple onion skins. Green – spinach. Blue – blueberries. **Tip**: Placing the eggs in a nylon stocking with the dye choice will intensify the color. Adding 1 tbsp. (15 mL) vinegar to each color of egg dye mixture, also intensifies the colors.

- As a substitute for place cards for Easter brunch, hard-boil the correct number of eggs and write each guest's name on the shells.
- Never eat a decorated egg if it has been kept out of the fridge for more than 2 hours (this includes hard-boiled eggs).
- Styrofoam egg cartons work well as packing material because they act as shock absorbers when lining a box that is to be shipped.
- Empty egg cartons may be recycled into: paint trays for kids, seedling starters, button holders, earring, pill and game piece organizers. **Note**: Save egg cartons for local daycare centers or bring cartons to neighbors who raise chickens. Who knows, you may be treated to a dozen free eggs.
- Even with today's technological advances in dishwashers, eggs are still the number one enemy of clean dishes. Baked-on egg should be sprinkled with dishwasher detergent and left to soak. Rinse well and scrape.
- After the eggs have been used and the shells remain, use them to give your thermos a thorough cleaning. Dry the eggshells and crush them with a rolling pin. Place the shells in a thermos with a little water and shake well.

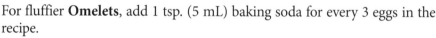 For fluffier **Omelets**, add 1 tsp. (5 mL) baking soda for every 3 eggs in the recipe.

EGGSTRA SECRETS

- **Soufflé**: The secret to success is producing stable egg white foam. No egg yolk can slip in. Use a glass or metal mixing bowl, never use plastic. Over time, the porous plastic will absorb impurities preventing egg from whipping properly.
- Perfect soufflé foam should be beaten until stiff. Egg whites must have a glossy, smooth and moist appearance. Don't open the oven door until 5 minutes before soufflé is ready. Never add egg yolks directly to a hot sauce, they may become lumpy. Stir a small amount of the egg yolks a little at a time.
- A soufflé is ready when the top is gold and feels firm to touch and jiggles only slightly when gently shaken.
- To steady deviled eggs on a plate, cut a thin slice off the bottom.
- Refrigerate eggs immediately to keep their freshness. Store in the carton to prevent moisture loss and odor absorption. Store away from strong smelling foods, Store yolks and whites in airtight containers.

The Meat that Meets your Standards

- Meat is one of the most expensive items on a grocery list. While filet mignon may win a popularity contest, top sirloin is an underrated choice that is lean, firm, tasty and less expensive. The trick when preparing sirloin is to leave just enough of the exterior fat to bring out the beefy flavor.

- **Where beef cuts come from**? At the top of the animal, starting near the head and going back toward the tail, are chuck, rib, short loin, sirloin and round. Underneath the animal, from front to back, are brisket, plate and flank. The tenderness of the cut depends on how much the animal has had to use the muscle. Therefore, cuts near the shoulder or leg, which are used often for movement, are going to be tougher. Muscles that are not used as much, in the center of the animal, include the rib, plate and loin. These are cooked in different ways to maximize flavor and tenderness. When preparing meat, make sure you remove the membrane on the underside of the ribs with a sharp knife. If you don't it blocks the flavor.

- Fat is flavor! A good cut of meat will have specks of white fat evenly distributed through the meat. Leaner cuts of beef, such as flank and round, have less fat and can benefit from marinades and dry rubs.

- To slice raw meat into thin strip for stir-fries, partially freeze; to slice easily.

 Kitchen Secret: T-Bone is an excellent steak for grilling. It has marbling (fat) that gives it flavor. It grills easily and is tender; just give it a rub with olive oil, then sprinkle it lightly with garlic salt before grilling.

- **Dry Heat Cooking Methods**: Lesser-used muscles are tender and do well with dry heat. Tender cuts of meat from the loin and rib are best suited for dry heat cooking methods such as grilling, broiling, roasting and sautéing.

- **Moist Heat Cooking Methods**: Frequently used muscles are tough and generally require long, slow, moist heat cooking methods to loosen their connective tissue. Moist heat cooking methods include braising, boiling and stewing. Tougher cuts of meat from the round, brisket, flank, plate, shank and chuck are best suited for moist heat cooking methods. The pressure-cooker is the perfect cooking appliance for braising and pot-roasting, steaming, poaching and stewing.

- Less expensive cuts of meat tend to be tougher. **Braising and stewing** are the most popular methods of softening tougher cuts of meat. What is braising? After browning, the meat is boiled then slowly simmered in a stock, usually accompanied with seasonings.

- **Roasts** should be allowed to "rest" 10-15 minutes after being removed from the oven. This allows the juices to settle before carving.

Kitchen Secret: Always use tongs to handle meat once it's on the grate. Don't pierce the meat and let the flavor ooze out.

- If you're going to baste during cooking stay away from anything with sugar in it. Your best bet is to use vinegar and/or water-based products only.
- Only spread barbecue sauce in the last few minutes of cooking. Any sooner and the heat will cause the sauce to caramelize and burn.
- Meat that has been marinated should be wiped dry before searing to form a second skin.

 Kitchen Secrets: Avoid flipping meat more than once; this may cause the meat to become dry.

- If a marinade calls for cornstarch, add it last. It will act as a binder.
- Always cut beef across the grain. This helps make it more tender.
- Cut the meat into uniform pieces so that it will cook evenly.
- A roast with the bone in will cook faster than a boneless roast because the bone carries the heat to the inside of the roast more quickly.
- Don't salt meat before you cook it. The salt forces the juices out and hinders browning. Instead, salt meat halfway through cooking, then taste when the meat is done and adjust the salt as needed.
- When making **meatloaf** put chili sauce or ranch dressing mix (dry powder type) in the meatloaf mix for terrific flavor.

 Kitchen Secret: To absorb the grease during cooking, put a slice of bread at each end of the meatloaf and cook as usual. Make **meatloaf in a ring mold** for a change. Fill the center with your favorite vegetable.

 Chef's Secret: For perfectly shaped **meatballs** scoop the meat with a tablespoon, this will aid in creating uniform meatballs every time.

- When forming **meatballs**, keep hands wet to keep the meat mixture from sticking. To make meatballs of uniform size, form mixture into a rectangle about 1" (2.5 cm) thick on waxed paper. Cut evenly into 1" (2.5 cm) cubes then form into meatballs.
- For a juicy **hamburger** add cold water to the beef before grilling. Ratio is ½ cup (125 mL) water to 1 lb. (500 g) of meat. For perfectly shaped patties, use a Tupperware hamburger press.
- Purchase **ribs** that are evenly covered in meat. Don't buy a slab that is fatty on one end and fleshy on the other. Avoid slabs that have exposed bones.
- Compare **turkey and chicken breasts**, the price difference during certain months is worth your attention. After Thanksgiving you will find turkey breasts priced less than hamburger. **Tip**: Frozen ground turkey is often one-third the price of fresh.
- Poultry should be roasted at 325°F (180°C) or higher to avoid food safety problems.

> **DID YOU KNOW?** Colonel Sanders was 65, when he set out (with his first $100.00 social security cheque, recipe and chicken fryer) on a journey across the U.S., knocking on restaurant doors, asking people to try his secret recipe. More then 1,000 companies rejected him. Yet, he didn't give up and finally received an order. Today, Kentucky Fried Chicken has 11,815 restaurants worldwide with annual retail sales of $9.7 billion, serving nearly 8-million customers a day.
>
> *Moral of the story ... don't give up on your dreams.*

- To improve the flavor of poultry, rub the inside and out with salt before roasting.
- When the label on chicken says, "air chilled" this mean the air has been forced out and the meat is high quality.
- To absorb chicken grease, set the chicken on a brown paper bag.
- When frying chicken, never allow more than ½" (1.3 cm) of fat in the skillet. Cover the skillet for the first 20 minutes of cooking to help keep the top of the chicken moist. Never turn frying chicken more than once and don't fiddle with the drumsticks. Use a pancake turner to flip fragile breaded foods in the skillet. Tongs might shatter the crust.
- For the crispiest-crusted fried chicken ever, roll the chicken in buttermilk, then in self-rising flour mixed with a little paprika and freshly ground black pepper.
- To tell if oil is hot enough for frying, place the tip of a large wooden spoon on the bottom of the wok or deep-fat fryer. If bubbles rise briskly around the end of the spoon the instant you insert it, the oil is ready to use. Do the spoon test many times as the oil gradually comes up to frying temperature.
- To bread chicken cutlets and other ingredients, use one hand for wet ingredients and another for dry; your hands will stay clean(er).
- To coat chicken pieces or stew-meat in flour or crumbs, place the coating mixture in a plastic bag (self-sealing is the most convenient), add the chicken or beef, seal and shake until coated. Shake off any excess coating before you cook the meat.
- It's important to let roast beef, pork, lamb or poultry sit a while before carving. This allows the juices to retreat back into the meat. If you carve a roast too soon, much of its goodness will spill out onto the carving board.
- Thaw and marinate meats in the refrigerator, not at room temperature.
- Remove excess fat from meat and poultry before placing in a slow cooker. During cooking, fat will liquefy and float to the top, so if not trimmed from the meat prior to cooking, you may want to skim it off afterwards. Always brown meat (especially ground meat) and drain the fat before placing it in the slow cooker.

Fishy Friends with Flavor

- Fresh fish should be stored in your refrigerator for only 1-2 days; it's very perishable. Any longer than that and wrap the fish well in freezer paper and freeze it. Keep it frozen until you're ready to cook it. Fish can be thawed in the refrigerator, under cold running water or in the microwave. Be sure to cook it as soon as it's thawed.

- Scale a fish easily by rubbing vinegar over its skin. To bake a whole fish, wrap in aluminum foil. When done cooking, open the foil and gently slide a spatula under the fish.

- To keep a cooked fish warm while you make the sauce, smooth wax paper over the fish and keep in a warm oven.

- Poaching fish involves cooking it gently in a simmering liquid (bouillon, milk, salted water, etc.). This method of cooking is particularly good for firm fillets and small whole fish.

- To determine how long to cook fish, measure the thickest part of the fish and cook it for 6-8 minutes per ½" (1.3 cm) in a 425°F (220°C) oven.

- Cooking fish with the bones intact makes for juicier and more flavorful fillets. Boning is easier than it seems and looks impressive at the table.

- To bone a cooked fish grasp the tail end of the backbone and remove it by slowly lifting it up and off the fish. Run a spoon or butter knife down the line where the backbone used to be. Use tweezers to pull off remaining small bones.

- To keep breading on food during frying, add ½ tsp. (2 mL) of sugar to the batter.

- To remove the smell of fish on your hands, rub with lemon juice, vinegar or salt. Washing with shampoo or rubbing with toothpaste are other tricks.

- Fillets are the hardest part of the fish to grill, the problem is that fish fillets tend to stick to the grill and crumble when turned. The secret is to use a fish or vegetable grill with lots of small holes that fits on top of the main grill. The grill holds the fillet flat so that pieces won't fall between the bars when you turn them.

- Cook fish on an oiled grill, skin side down for the first part of the cooking time. The skin protects the fish from burning and drying out. It can also provide natural oils so when you flip the fish it doesn't stick to the grills.

- To ensure that fish does not shrivel up as it cooks, make small incisions in the skin or in the thin layer of nerve tissue beneath the skin.

- Fish is cooked when the flesh flakes easily with a fork and appears opaque all the way through. If any of the flesh is still glossy and translucent then it is not done. Test for doneness; if skin looks opaque, fish should flake easily. Shellfish must be firm and white.

- Shrimp that have been peeled and deveined before freezing lose flavor and texture. Shrimp should not be overcooked or they will become tough and lose their sweet flavor. It usually takes about 3 minutes to cook them. When shrimp turn pink, they are done. Also, when shrimp curl into a semicircle they're done. When tightly coiled, they're overdone.

 Kitchen Secret: Keeping shellfish fresh can be tricky. Crabs and lobsters will keep an extra 1-2 days wrapped in damp newspapers and stored in the refrigerator. Oysters, clams and mussels should be wrapped very tightly in a mesh or perforated bag, weighted down and put in the fridge. This method (by preventing them from opening and spilling their juices) maintains their quality and extends their life.

Dear Reena,

Have you ever heard of soaking thawed frozen fish in salt or vinegar prior to cooking to get rid of the "fishy smell"? The only person in my family who is not dairy intolerant is me so I stay away from milk in my cooking. Sincerely Tova

Tova,

Have I got a list for you? Begin by choosing fish with a minimal odor such as Halibut, Mahi Mahi, Basa, Talapia, Snapper, Cod or Pollock. Any fish that has a very fishy odor should not be eaten, as fresh fish does not have a strong odor. Since you are dairy intolerant, soaking the fish in milk for 30 minutes will not be an option for you. Instead use a citrus-based marinade such as lemon, lime or orange or place the fruit directly into the pan while baking. This enhances the fish flavor as well as the odor. Do not soak fish in a citrus-based marinade for more than 2 hours, as the acid will begin to break down the cellular structure of the fish.

Other options include: soaking the fish in vinegar, sprinkling with baking soda, poaching the fish in white wine or putting 7-Up or a can of Sprite into a zip-loc bag along with the fish before freezing.

What's the Word on Tea?

- The key to brewing iced tea is to make it double strength and use twice as many leaves (rather than steep the tea for twice the time). If you allow the tea to steep for too long, it will get bitter. Teas to use for iced tea: include black, green, white, Oolong, Pu-erh and herbal.

- Before making tea note that water quality affects taste. If your tap water has additives such as chlorine or fluoride, consider using spring water.

- All true tea, comes from the leaves of a tree called Camellia sinensis. The leaves of this tree are picked and then "withered" or wilted. Steaming the leaves at this point prevents oxidization (a process in which the leaf's enzymes come in contact with the oxygen in the air).

- Decide which form of tea you will use. Most bag teas are a lower quality than loose leaves. However, there are some quality bagged teas available.

- Before pouring tea into teapots, fill the pots with hot water and let sit for a few moments, drain. Doing this will keep the tea hot longer.

- Let tea steep from 2-5 minutes, depending on the type of tea and strength that you prefer. Large leaves require more steeping time than small ones.

- Tea contains less caffeine per cup than coffee; if you are sensitive to caffeine you can decaffeinate tea by allowing tea to steep half a minute; pour off the water. Immediately add fresh, boiling water to the wet tea leaves; steep 2-5 minutes as usual. Tea's caffeine is released within the first minute of steeping.

- When serving tea, offer sugar and lemon or milk (never cream it is too heavy and masks the flavor of the tea).

- When serving lemon with tea, use slices, not wedges. Provide a small fork or lemon fork for your guests, or have the tea server place a slice in the teacup after the tea has been poured. Be sure never to add lemon with milk since the lemon's citric acid will cause the proteins in the milk to curdle. Studies have shown that green tea has many health benefits including rich anti-oxidants, cancer-prevention, breath freshener and anti-aging properties.

- When using loose tea, allow for 1 tsp. (5 mL) tea to 1 cup (250 mL) of water or 1 tsp. (5 mL) of leaves per person, plus 1 further tsp. (5 mL) "for the pot." The leaves can be added to the pot or put in an infuser. If they are loose, you need to strain the liquid as it goes into the cup. Add 1 tea bag for every 1-2 cups (250-500 mL) water, depending on preference.

- A tea infuser or teaball holds loose tea leaves for brewing. When using an infuser fill it only halfway so that the wet leaves can expand.

Household Solutions 2 with Kitchen Secrets

- Common herbs used in teas include:
  - **Chamomile**: Used to treat many digestive issues, cramps, nausea, diarrhea, fever, congestion, headaches, insomnia and stress.
  - **Anise**: Licorice flavored tea used for digestive issues, coughs and congestion.
  - **Lemongrass**: May help decrease cholesterol levels. It can also help with coughing, bladder problems, digestive issues, headaches, fever; it also promotes perspiration.
  - **Mint**: Mint is extremely easy to grow and hardy (it may actually take over your garden). It is a great herb to make into a tea for digestive problems; a smart choice before bed.

Coffee is Sooo Much More than a Drink!

- Coffee is the most consumed beverage in the world. Coffee beans originated in Ethiopia and in some African tribes, they ate the beans to enhance their strength before venturing into battles.

- Some people are passionate about the flavor of coffee and prefer to stick with one brand. Before choosing to be brand loyal, allow yourself a blindfolded taste test and decide whether or not you really notice a difference.

 To make **Iced Coffee**: Brew 1 pot of coffee, single or double strength and transfer to a carafe. Let stand at room temperature for 3-5 hours (or refrigerate until cold). Fill a glass with ice cubes and pour chilled coffee into the glass. Add milk and sweetener to taste. **Tip**: Stir sweetened condensed milk into warm coffee before pouring it over ice.

- When preparing coffee, use 2 tbsp. (30 mL) ground coffee per 6 oz. (170 g) of water. Adjust for personal taste.

- Water has the greatest impact on coffee flavor. Always start with cool water. Don't use distilled water; which lacks the minerals that gives coffee flavor.

- Using stainless steel or gold mesh paper filters will make coffee taste better. If you use paper filters, buy unbleached brown paper filters. Prevent coffee grounds from dropping into the coffee pot by wetting the filter before making coffee.

- Flavoring syrups, cold milk, chocolate and spices allow you to create your own personalized coffee concoctions.

Solutions 2

How to Choose from the Most Popular Cheeses

Labels on natural cheese, pasteurized process cheese and related products carry important information. The name of a natural cheese will appear as the variety, such as Cheddar, Swiss or Blue cheese.

Pasteurized process cheese labels always include the words "pasteurized process," with the name of the variety or varieties of cheese used for, e.g., "pasteurized process American cheese" or "pasteurized process Swiss cheese."

Cheese food contains ingredients other than cheese and is labeled as "pasteurized process cheese food." Cheese spreads have a different composition and are labeled as "pasteurized process cheese spread." All ingredients are listed on the labels, along with the kinds or varieties of cheese used in the mixture. Also, the milk fat and moisture content may be shown.

The age or degree of curing is important label information on certain varieties of natural cheese. For example, Cheddar cheese may be labeled as "mild," "medium" or "mellow," and "aged" or "sharp." In some cases, pasteurized process cheese may be labeled to indicate a sharp flavor when a much higher amount of sharp or aged cheese was used in its preparation. The harder the cheese, the higher the fat.

- **BLUE CHEESE:** The longer blue cheese is aged the firmer and more intense tasting it becomes. To serve, remove blue cheese from packaging and warm to room temperature, to give the cheese a chance to breathe and release its flavor.

- **BRIE:** Soften at room temperature and serve on crackers or with fresh fruit. Heated Brie melts into an elegant spread for crackers, croissant and crusty breads. Brie ripens from the outside in not the inside out.

- **CREAM CHEESE:** Soft, white, smooth, it spreads easily and melts quickly. Mild and slightly acidic, often flavored with fruits or herbs, it is a wonderful addition to many desserts. Serve with fresh fruit, jams and jellies, fruit, nut breads and bagels.

- **FETA:** The intense flavor of feta enhances the flavor and texture of salads, especially when combined with olives, tomatoes and a variety of greens, including fresh spinach. In salt brine it can be stored almost indefinitely. To decrease its saltiness you can soak the cheese in spring water or milk for a few minutes before serving.

- **FONTINA**: A very pale Italian yellow, creamy cow's milk cheese with a mild flavor. Fontina goes well with crackers and makes an excellent addition to macaroni and cheese because it melts so well.

- **GOAT CHEESE** (CHÈVRE): Should look moist. Reject if air-bloated, moldy or leaking whey. To store, protect the cheese from air with the original wrappings, plastic wrap or waxed paper. Remove from refrigerator 1 hour before serving. Freeze for longer storage. All goat cheeses are heat sensitive and when overheated will become grainy and separate. When using in recipes, heat until just melted. Spread on toast or bagels, use in dips, top green salads with crumbled cheese or with slices warmed in oven.

- **GRUYÈRE**: A nutty, pale yellow, firm cow's milk cheese. This cheese can be stored for more than a month and is ideal for fondues, topping potatoes, zucchini, asparagus and in French onion soup.

- **MASCARPONE**: Made from the milk of cows that have been fed special grasses filled with fresh herbs and flowers, this cheese has a unique taste, often described as "fresh and delicious." Mascarpone can be layered in tiramisu or used as a filling in desserts such as tarts and cheesecake. The fat content of the cheese adds to the richness of pasta sauces.

- **MONTEREY JACK CHEESE**: A somewhat soft, white melting cheese with a mild flavor and buttery texture, it is made from whole, partly skimmed or skimmed cow's milk. Jack cheese is a great choice for breakfast tacos (scrambled eggs, chopped tomatoes, shredded lettuce and cheese), bean-and-cheese nachos (tortilla chips spread with refried beans and shredded, melted cheese) and broiled open-face sandwiches.

- **PARMESAN**: Can be served as a table cheese; Parmesan also makes a great accompaniment to pasta, fruits and bread. Fresh Parmesan should be wrapped in parchment or waxed paper and then in aluminum foil, before it is refrigerated; it can then be kept for several weeks. Grated Parmesan can be stored for longer periods; in a tightly closed container in the freezer. **Tip:** Purchasing pre-grated cheese may cost up to 70% more than a block of cheese.

 Kitchen Secret: Store a sugar cube with cheese to keep it from hardening.

 Kitchen Secret: To make blue cheese, mozzarella and other soft cheeses easier to grate, place them in the freezer for about 20 minutes.

 Kitchen Secret: Purchase cream cheese on sale in bulk and freeze. Milk and whip cream may also be frozen. *Submitted by Ladine Dyck.*

Flours

Common types of flour: Flour is a milled and finely ground starch product that can be produced from a variety of different edible grains or vegetables. Wheat is the most common source of flour used for cooking.

- **ALL-PURPOSE FLOUR**: Has medium protein content and blended wheat flour suitable for most household baking needs. Store all-purpose flour in an airtight container for up to 1 year.

- **To bleach or not to bleach**? All-purpose flour is the same whether bleached or unbleached, bleaching makes for whiter baked goods. Some people prefer unbleached because they don't like the thought of a baked good with a bleaching agent in it (even if it's just a small amount). Flours treated with these bleaching agents must be labeled as bleached. If a recipe doesn't specify, you can use either one, but where a whiter color is desired, use the bleached one.

- Enriched all-purpose flour has iron and B-vitamins added in amounts equal to or exceeding that of whole-wheat flour. Enriched/fortified bread is made from enriched white flour, which is milled from only the endosperm of the wheat kernel. Enrichment causes no change in taste, color, texture or caloric value and each slice contains nearly 1 gram of fiber.

- **BREAD FLOUR**: Weighs in between 12% and 13% protein, and helps produce wonderfully well-risen, chewy loaves of bread. Bread flour has more gluten and protein than all-purpose flour; this is the best choice for yeast products. Whole-wheat flour made from the whole kernel of wheat is normally not the main ingredient in baked products; it is heavy which keeps baked goods from rising. If choosing to use make a loaf of whole wheat bread, increase the water content and knead for a longer amount of time. Whole-wheat flour is higher in fiber and nutrition than all of the white flours. In England whole wheat is known as whole meal flour. Whole-wheat flour has a shorter shelf life than white, store in the fridge or freezer.

- Not all wheat breads are the same. Look at the ingredients; whole-wheat flour should be listed first. Whole wheat bread has the entire wheat kernel and all the

nutrients that naturally occur in wheat. If the ingredient listed is wheat flour, this is not whole grain bread. Only part of the wheat kernel is used to make this flour. The brown color of wheat bread comes from adding color like molasses.

- **INSTANT FLOUR**: Is not a good substitute for all-purpose or cake flour. It dissolves quickly in hot and cold water and used mainly for sauces and gravies.

- **CAKE FLOUR**: Has the least amount of gluten of all wheat flours which makes it perfect for sponge cakes, muffins, genoise, quick breads and cookies. When baking with a high sugar to flour ratio, cake flour is less liable to collapse. Cake flour has high starch content and is low in protein.

- **PASTRY FLOUR**: Is made with soft wheat and is quite low in protein and is often used in making biscuits, brownies, quick breads, cookies, pie crusts, and pastries. Will not work for yeast breads but makes a tender, crumbly pastry.

- **Cake flour and pastry flour:** Are both milled from soft wheat which has a lower gluten and protein content meaning that the dough have less strength and ability to stretch. Pizza dough made with pastry dough stretches easily due to the high gluten content as apposed to if you make a cake it is impossible to stretch that. Cake Flour is used for cakes and other delicate baked goods that require low gluten content. Pastry flour is stronger than cake flour. It has the same creamy white color as bread flour, not the pure white of cake flour.

- **What is GLUTEN**? A mixture of plant proteins found in cereal grains, mainly corn and wheat, used as an adhesive and as a flour substitute.

- **SELF-RISING FLOUR** (phosphated flour): Is low-protein flour with salt and leavening already added. Read the ingredients or a recipe, salt and baking soda can be left out when using self-rinsing. This works well for quick breads and biscuits not for yeast breads.

- **SEMOLINA FLOUR**: Is made from durum wheat. Semolina is the coarsely ground prime endosperm of durum wheat, is high in protein and used in making couscous, highest quality pasta, rolled pasta dough and semolina gnocchi.

- **DURUM FLOUR**: Is made from durum wheat, is the hardest wheat grown and is a by-product in the production of semolina. High in protein and gluten strength, durum is good for some pastas and specialty breads. Do not use for cakes.

- **ORGANIC FLOUR**: Is used the same as regular flour. It must follow agriculture regulations to be labeled "organic." It is a matter of personal preference.

ORGANICALLY GROWN

- **What does "organic" mean?** "Organic" implies that no (or minimal) commercial fertilizers or pesticides were used to produce or store the food. Organic agricultural practices promote sustainable growing methods that nurture the soil, crops and animals, creating a beneficial habitat for all living things. In addition, consumers who purchase organically grown foods may benefit from the flavor of foods grown and harvested with care, in healthy soil.

- **GLUTEN-FREE FLOUR**: Is high in protein and low in starch. Use it for diabetic or gluten-free breads, or mixed with other non-wheat flours to create strong dough. It is made from wheat endosperm treated to remove starch. Bread made with gluten flour is dry, fine-grained, and somewhat tough and becomes stale quickly. Dough made of flours low in gluten can be improved by replacing 5-10% of the flour with gluten flour. On the other hand, gluten flour can be used in a 2:1 ratio with wheat flour. Decrease normal kneading time to avoid overdeveloping the gluten. Bake at a higher temperature to keep color in the bread. Store gluten flour in a dry area.

 Kitchen Secret: When working with dough, don't flour your hands; coat them with olive oil to prevent sticking.

Guide to Sweeteners

- Standing in front of the candy shelf at the local grocery store, I was amazed by the selection. Every chocolate bar under the sun, how would I ever decide? Before taking one more step, I glanced at a package of chocolate that displayed the words I had been waiting all of my life to hear, "Delicious sugar-free chocolate" and the best part was that it was produced by one of my very favorite chocolate-making companies. I quickly turned over the bag to study the packaging. My smile immediately turned upside down when I looked at the ingredients and listed first was the word "maltose." Oh, I thought, I knew it was too good to be true. Of course, maltose is another name for sugar, (malt sugar) and when I read the caloric information it all made sense.

- Sugar, once a luxury, is now an inexpensive, easily accessible commodity. The most common forms of sugar are granulated white, brown and confectioner's. Commercial sugar comes from sugar cane (a tropical plant and a member of the grass family) and sugar beets

> **SWEET TRIVIA:**
> Sugar is the most common ingredient added to processed foods today and consumption is on the rise.

- **Granulated White Sugar** contains almost 99% pure sucrose. It is a highly refined sweetener that has most of the original flavor and compounds removed during processing. Organic unbleached varieties are a healthier choice.

- **Confectioner's (icing/powdered) Sugar** is typically used in baking and a key ingredient in icing recipes. It is made from crushed granulated white sugar with a small amount of cornstarch to keep it from clumping. You can substitute 1 cup (250 mL) of granulated sugar and 1 tsp. (5 mL) cornstarch for 1¾ cups (425 mL) confectioner's sugar. Blend well.

- **Brown Sugar**: There are 2 basic types, sticky and free flowing. Both are produced by adding a suitable type of syrup (these days it's usually molasses) to purified or refined sugar. The color and texture of the final product are determined by the ratio of sugar to syrup in the mix, as well the original colors of the constituent ingredients. Unrefined brown sugar contains 85-98% sucrose. Substituting brown for white sugar will make baking more moist. You can substitute 1 cup (250 mL) granulated sugar for 1 cup (250 mL) brown sugar.

- **Unrefined Sugar**: Produced from raw sugar, it has naturally occurring nutrients, flavor and color. Maple syrup, raw honey, barley malt and rice syrup are unrefined sweeteners.
- **Demerara**: A coarse-ground, medium-brown sugar with a crunchy texture and a mild molasses flavor. Use to decorate cakes or topping on desserts.
- **Dark Muscovado**: With a high molasses content and a moist texture, it works well in gingerbread and cookies.
- **Turbinado**: Similar to Demerara but a little more refined, use it in baking, on oatmeal or in coffee. Substitute 1 cup (250 mL) granulated white sugar for 1 cup (250 mL) turbinado sugar. Turbinado sugar is typically used as a less "stinging" alternative to salt in scrub recipes. Larger, uniform light brown grains give a unique earthy look to body care formulas.
- **Molasses**: Produced during the sugar refining process, the syrup remains after the sucrose has been crystallized from the cane juice. Light molasses is the first boiling of the cane; dark molasses is from the second; blackstrap from the third. Molasses can be sulfured or unsulfured. Sulfured is the by-product of the sugar-making process where fumes used in manufactured sugar are retained. Unsulfured is a more popular choice. Molasses is used in baking gingerbread and spicy treats. Substitute 1 cup granulated white sugar for 1 cup (250 mL) molasses (reduce liquid by 4 tsp./20 mL for EACH 1 cup/ 250 mL) used. Dark molasses is most popular for baking; blackstrap molasses is quite bitter. It is used as cattle feed and was a popular health food.
- **Maple Syrup**: Boiled down tree sap of the sugar maple, it consists of 62% sucrose, about 60% as sweet as sugar. Maple sugar is made by boiling the sap until the liquid has evaporated. Maple syrup and maple sugar are very refined sweeteners.
- Pure maple syrup is graded according to color and flavor, the highest being AA. As a substitute for sugar the A or AA graded syrup is the best choice. Honey and maple syrup work interchangeably in recipes, use the same amount. Substitute 1 cup (250 mL) white granulated sugar for ¾ cup (175 mL) maple syrup (reduce liquid in recipe by 3 tbsp./45 mL).
- **Barley Malt and Rice Syrup**: Made from soaked and sprouted barley, which is then dried and cooked down to thick syrup, barley malt is a sweetener that is slowly digested and as a result is gentler on blood sugar levels

than other sweeteners. Rice syrup is a combination of rice and barley. Both sweeteners contain significant quantities of the sugar maltose, which causes a slower rising of blood sugar levels. Substitute 1 cup (250 mL) white granulated sugar for ¾ cup (175 mL) barley malt or rice syrup (reduce liquid in recipe by ¼ cup/60 mL).

- **BEWARE!** Manufacturers purposely split up the names of sugars on ingredient lists found on food and beverages so that the consumer does not realize how much sweetener is in a product. Ingredients lists must be in order from the greatest quantity ingredient to the least, therefore, an item will often be made with brown sugar as well as white sugar. By using 2 different types of sugars the sugar content is split up so that sugar is not listed first and can instead be listed third or fourth. By the way, white sugar is made up of 50% glucose and 50% fructose. READ THE LABEL!

- **OTHER NAMES FOR SUGARS AND SWEETENERS:**

  - Fructose
  - HFCS (high fructose corn syrup)
  - Sucrose
  - Glucose
  - Regular Corn Syrup
  - Maltose
  - Galactose
  - Lactose (sugar present in milk)
  - High Conversion Corn Syrup
  - Regular Conversion Corn Syrup
  - Invert Sugar
  - Sorbitol
  - Xylitol
  - Saccharin
  - Sucrol (dulcin)
  - Honey
  - Molasses
  - Sorghum Syrup
  - Dextrose (glucose sugar refined from cornstarch)
  - Maltose/Malt Sugar/Diglucose (Carbohydrate typically used in infant formulas and beer)
  - Maltodextrin (Carbohydrate made from cornstarch)
  - Aspartame
  - Acesulfame K
  - Alitame
  - Sucralose
  - Galactitol
  - Malitol
  - Lactitol
  - Cyclamate
  - Dihydrochalcones
  - Glycyrrhizin
  - L-sugars
  - Mannitol
  - Monellin
  - Stevioside
  - Talin

Fats

- Which is healthier, butter or margarine?

- **Butter** is a natural product made from milk, like other animal products, butter contains saturated fat. The down side is that saturated fat consumption raises blood cholesterol levels and causes inflammation in arteries and other parts of the body.

- Originally, **margarine** was manufactured to fatten turkeys but the turkeys died. The investors who had put all the money into the research wanted a way to redeem their money and market the margarine.

- The best cooking oils have a lower EFA content (polyunsaturated) and a higher percentage of mono-saturated and saturated fats. Oils such as olive oil and canola may actually benefit the heart. For great flavor choose: extra-virgin olive, sesame, peanut or walnut oil. Corn, safflower and sunflower oils are high in polyunsaturated fats (good when used in moderation). Boost your omega-3 fatty acids by choosing walnut oil. Remember, all oils are high in fat, so use sparingly. **Tip**: For deep-fat frying, choose oils that won't burn easily, e.g., corn, safflower, super canola and soy work well. Be careful with nut oils – check to see if your guests have nut allergies before using.

- Margarine is made from polyunsaturated vegetable oils such as corn oil. These vegetable oils don't contain any saturated fats like animal products, so margarine was deemed to be "heart healthy." At the time margarine became popular it was not known that the margarine making process turns polyunsaturated oils into semi-solid margarine and also creates trans fats.

- Both butter and margarine should be used in small amounts but, overall, butter is a good choice because there is room for a small amount of saturated fats in our diet, but trans fats need to be kept almost to zero.

- Another option is non-hydrogenated margarine which contains no trans fatty acids, but read the label. Not all margarines are non-hydrogenated. Buy non-hydrogenated soft margarine. Look for brands made primarily with canola oil or olive oil. Both are heart-healthy monounsaturated fats.

 Chef's Secret: Serve guests butter balls using a small melon baller. Roll the balls in crushed herbs or ground paprika for color; arrange on a serving dish and refrigerate before serving.

- Saturated fats are most often of animal origin (solid at room temperature). Examples of foods high in saturated fats include lard, butter, whole milk, cream, eggs, red meat, chocolate and solid shortenings.

- **Trans fats** are artificial fats created when hydrogen gas reacts with oil. They can be found in cookies, crackers, icing, potato chips, margarine and microwave popcorn. Manufacturers include trans fats in processed foods to prolong shelf life. Numerous studies have concluded that trans fats raise heart disease risk. They raise total cholesterol levels and deplete good cholesterol (HDL), which helps protect against heart disease.

- **Monounsaturated fatty acids** contain one double bond. Examples of foods high in monounsaturated fat include avocados, nuts and olive, canola and peanut oils. Scientists believe that monounsaturated fats are helpful in lowering LDL (bad) cholesterol and lowering the risk of heart disease.

- **Polyunsaturated fats** include the healthy omega-3 fatty acids, they are found in plant oils such as safflower, sunflower, corn, soy, flaxseed and canola oils, as well as in seafood. They are either liquid or soft at room temperature.

- **Essential fatty acids** are polyunsaturated fatty acids that the human body needs for metabolic functioning but cannot produce, so acquires it from foods.

- **Omega-3 fatty acids** are a class of essential polyunsaturated fatty acids. Foods high in omega-3-fatty acids include salmon, halibut, sardines, albacore, trout, herring, walnut, flaxseed oil and canola oil. Other foods that contain omega-3-fatty acids include: shrimp, clams, light chunk tuna, catfish, cod and spinach.

- **Omega-6 fatty acids** are a class of essential polyunsaturated fatty acids. Examples of foods rich in omega-6 fatty acids include corn, flaxseed, pumpkin seed oil, sesame oil, hemp oil, safflower oil, sunflower, soybean and cottonseed oil.

 Kitchen Secret: To get the full benefits of flax seed in recipes or on cereals, grind it in a coffee grinder.

- **What are Mono and Diglycerides?** These are substances often found in foods such as ice cream, margarine, instant potatoes and chewing gum. They are fats that are made from oil, usually soybean, cottonseed, sunflower or palm oil and act as emulsifiers (provide a consistent texture and prevent separation). Glycerides are used in baked products to keep them from becoming stale. They do not contain gluten.

- **Important!** Fat-free cakes, cookies and ice cream may have as much added sugars as their fatty counterparts and are often high in calories. "Fat-Free" on the label does not mean fat-free in your body.

- **Triglycerides** are fats carried in the blood from the food we eat. Excess calories, alcohol or sugar in the body are converted into triglycerides and stored in fat cells throughout the body. The more fat you eat, the higher your triglycerides jump.

 Kitchen Secret: Products that last more then 90 days do not need a best before date.

 Kitchen Secret: Drain deep-fried foods on brown paper grocery bags as opposed to paper towels to retain crispness.

Sodium

- The most popular spice in North America is salt. If every particle of salt was taken from our bodies, we would live about 48 hours. In other words, we can't survive without sodium, but it was about 5 million years before humans began to consume sodium as salt.

- Many people are trying to cut back on sodium due to high blood pressure. North Americans eat much more salt than is needed, but what stops some people from reducing their intake is that they don't realize what they are eating contains high amount of salt. Keep in mind, there are many alternate names for salt, reading the label may be confusing. Check the sodium content on the nutrition label. It will allow you to compare quantities of a variety of foods.

- Sodium Chloride is table salt. Other ingredients that contain sodium and play a variety of functions are:
    + **Sodium benzoate**: Prevents growth of bacteria. Found in acidic foods such as fruit juices, jams, relishes and drinks.
    + **Sodium bicarbonate (baking soda)**: A leavening agent that helps to release a gas in baked goods to produce increased volume and tenderness.
    + **Sodium caprate (sodium caprylate)**: A binder, emulsifier and anti-caking agent.
    + **Sodium caseinate**: Thickener and binder in coffee whiteners, non-dairy whipped toppings, meats and desserts.
    + **Sodium citrate**: Controls acidity, stability; aids in emulsification; improves rehydration of foods.
    + **Sodium erythorbate**: An antioxidant, prevents color and flavor changes.
    + **Sodium propionate**: A preservative and mold inhibitor in many foods.
    + **Sodium saccharin** (saccharin): An artificial sweetener.
    + **Sodium nitrite/nitrate**: Prevents bacterial growth and preserves food.
    + **Sodium sulfite** (sodium bisulfite, sodium metabisulfate): Prevents fruit from darkening and losing flavor and vitamins while it's being dried.
    + **Monosodium glutamate (MSG)**: A flavor enhancer. Chinese food often uses MSG; people with allergies can ask for no MSG.

- **Sodium phosphates**: Emulsifiers and stabilizers in processed cheese; improves texture in processed meats.

- **Sodium lactate, sodium diacetate**: Prevents growth of harmful bacteria in ready-to-eat meats.

Rice

- The most important rule when cooking rice, "never lift the lid." Rinse rice several times before you cook it – all types, until the water comes out clear. Some rice is coated with talc in processing. This material is inert and won't hurt when ingested. For fluffier, faster-cooking rice, soak it in cold water for 30-60 minutes.

- Use a little less water than the recipes call for if you want fluffy rice. The ratio of rice to water should be a little less than 1:2.

- Use **long-grain white rice** when cooking Asian food. **Medium-grain rice** is also acceptable, but chefs use **short-grain rice** mainly for dishes such as congee (rice porridge).

- **Converted rice** has been parboiled with the husks on. More nutritious than white rice, it is not as flavorful. It takes longer to cook than regular rice, so follow package instructions carefully.

- If rice is taking a long time to cook it may be old. Older rice can lose some of its moisture, requiring more water and a longer cooking time.

- Leftover rice will keep for days and is perfect for making fried rice. The rice must be cold before storing it in the refrigerator. For best results, wait a couple of days before making fried rice. To reheat rice, line a vegetable steamer with a coffee filter; warm over boiling water.

- For a bit of variety, try a scented rice such as **jasmine** or **basmati**. Just remember that the amount of water required and the cooking time will be less than for other types of long-grain white rice.

- **Risotto** results from a specific way of cooking short-grain rice; hot stock is added to the rice, a little at a time, as the rice absorbs it.

- After about 12 minutes of cooking rice, the liquid should be absorbed, the rice will be al dente. The top layer will be drier and fluffier than the bottom, which will be moist and fragile. Remove rice from heat and leave, undisturbed, with the lid on, for at least 5 minutes and for as long as 30. This results in a uniform texture, with the bottom layers as fluffy as the top.

 Kitchen Secret: Rice actually improves with a rest, giving you more flexibility for cooking the remainder of the meal. For a longer wait, place a slice of dry bread on the rice to keep it fluffy; cover.

- A bit of butter or olive oil will help keep the grains from sticking together, while a little salt adds flavor. Another way to add flavor to rice is by adding garlic, lemon juice and grated zest, curry or turmeric to the pot, or substitute chicken broth for the water.

Pasta Perfection!

- Contrary to popular belief, pasta does not cause you to gain weight (unless you eat too much of it); it does not raise cholesterol (unless tossed with highly saturated fats) and does not raise blood sugar (when eaten as part of a meal). The following guidelines will help you on your way to becoming a great Italian chef (or at least satisfy your family).
- Never combine 2 types of pasta in the same pot; they will not cook evenly.
- Add 1-2 tsp. (5-10 mL) salt per 1 lb (500 g) of pasta. Add salt only after the water boils. Salted water adds flavor to pasta.
- Cook a large quantity of pasta. When cooled, divide into individual servings and put into plastic bags. Freeze. When you want a quick meal, drop the contents of the bag into boiling water, drain and serve.
- Strengthen homemade pasta dough by substituting ½ cup (125 mL) of semolina flour in place of ½ cup (125 mL) all-purpose flour.
- Cook pasta in a pot that is large enough to accommodate pasta without crowding.

 Kitchen Secret: For 1 lb. (500 g) of pasta choose an 8-quart (8 L) pot.

- Bring the water to a boil before adding pasta. Pasta often sticks together because it releases natural starches that act like glue; this is less likely to occur in boiling water.
- After the pasta has been placed in boiling water, return the water to a boil. Do not cover the pot. Stir pasta gently every 3 minutes.
- Think twice before adding oil to the pot. Oil prevents the sauce from coating the pasta properly (if the pot is the right size, oil is unnecessary).
- Follow instructions when cooking pasta, but remember this is only a guideline. When pasta is almost ready, test every 15 seconds until properly cooked.
- Cooked pasta should always have a "soul," a little white dot at the center, when it is cooked to perfection, al dente.

WHAT IS AL DENTE?

ANSWER:
An Italian term literally meaning "to the tooth," used to describe pasta that is not overcooked or soft but with a bit of resistance in the bite.

- Never overcook pasta. Test pasta for doneness by pinching it under cold running water. To stop cooking immediately, blanch in cold water. Spaghetti can be stored in cold water, covered and refrigerated for up to 2 days. Before serving, reheat in boiling salted water, drain and serve.

 Kitchen Secret: When thrown against a wall, if pasta sticks, it is ready to serve.

- Drain pasta in a large colander and toss it to remove excess liquid. Pasta should remain moist, not soaking wet.

- Sauce the pasta immediately after draining. Use only enough sauce to coat the pasta.

- To salvage burnt tomato sauce, add 1 tsp. (5 mL) peanut butter.

 Kitchen Secret: Store spaghetti sauce upside down to create a seal and prevent mold.

- An easy way to eat spaghetti is by twirling it with a fork and a soup-size spoon. In the hand you normally eat with, hold the spoon. With the other hand, use the fork to spear several strands of pasta. Twirl the fork against the spoon; your noodles will be under control. This is frowned on in some places, as is cutting long strands of pasta, however, go with what makes life easier. OR, order penne, fusilli, tortellini, conchiglie (shells) or other short pasta.

 Kitchen Secret: A jar lid or a couple of marbles in the bottom half of a double-boiler will rattle when the water gets low and warn you to add more water before the pan scorches or burns.

 Kitchen Secret: Noodles, spaghetti and other starches won't boil over if you rub the inside of the pot with vegetable oil.

Ciao!

Outstanding Pizza Dough

- Homemade pizza dough is easier to make than you think, give it a try. You will save both time and money.

- Mix dough carefully to avoid adding too much flour. The moisture content of flours may vary, so slightly more or less flour may be needed to achieve the correct light, springy consistency. Too much flour can make heavy dough and dense or tough crust. Too little flour will make sticky dough, liable to tear during shaping. The ideal dough is soft, springy and pliable, but not rubbery.

- If you have trouble forming the pizza crust, the gluten may be the problem. Gluten gives the dough elasticity and tight dough wants to spring back into shape. Partially shape the crust and then walk away for 5-10 minutes. When you get back, the dough will have relaxed and you can finish the crust.

- Adding more toppings to the pizza increases moisture and mass to cook through. For example, a deluxe pizza with 4-5 different toppings generally requires a longer baking time at a lower temperature, perhaps 325-350°F (160-180°C) for 25-35 minutes. For regular topping pizzas bake at higher temperatures.

- Take your pizza to the next level; purchase a pizza stone and a peel. The peel is used to move the pizza in and out of the oven. The pizza stone cooks the pizza as a brick oven would. There is nothing like it! Another option is to use a pizza pan with holes in the bottom; this helps the crust to bake evenly.

- Olive oil makes a much nicer pizza crust than vegetable oil.

- An incredible way to cook pizza is grill it! Your pizza will come out with a flavor that cannot be beat!

- Sauté onions and peppers before putting them on the pizza.

- Pizza dough is different from bread dough; it is a simpler dough, only rises once while most breads require 2 proofs. Pizza dough has more texture and flavor.

- If your homemade pizza dough is soggy, prebake dough for 5 minutes before adding sauce and toppings.

- Put cornmeal on pizza crust to make the crust crisper.

- The difference between pizza dough and focaccia bread is that focaccia is thicker than pizza crust. It can be used either as a bread (for sandwiches, dips, etc.) or as a thick pizza crust.

 Kitchen Secret: If you are having trouble cutting pizza with a knife or pizza wheel, cut with kitchen shears.

Pie Crust You Can Be Proud Of

 Kitchen Secret: My friend Jane Ruddy, in her 90s, gave me the secret to great pie crusts. Don't over knead. The trick to make a perfect flaky pie crust is to handle or mix the dough as little as possible. When rolling it out you should still see flakes of butter. She used the recipe on the back of the Crisco box and every pie crust was delicious.

 An alternative **Pie Crust Recipe**:

> 3 cups (750 mL) sifted all-purpose flour
> 1 tsp. (5 mL) salt
> ½ cup (125 mL) vegetable oil
> 1 tbsp. (15 mL) vinegar
> ½ cup (125 mL) milk

Mix flour and salt together. Pour oil, vinegar and milk into a measuring cup, do not stir and add all at once to flour. Stir until mixed, divide dough into 2 flat balls. Wrap in plastic wrap. Refrigerate for 1 hour. Roll out on floured surface, with a floured rolling pin. **Makes enough pastry for 2 pies**.

- Dough can be refrigerated for 3 days or frozen for weeks. If frozen, thaw and bring to room temperature before rolling out crust.
- For a flaky crust, the butter and water must be ICE COLD! Put shortening in fridge for 30 minutes this will help make a flaky crust.
- Add the flour slowly, kneading with a pastry cutter.
- Add an extra tbsp. (15 mL) of vinegar to the dough; roll the dough between 2 pieces of waxed paper to prevent sticking and for easy transfer. Roll the dough from the center out, lifting the rolling pin at the edge. Make the dough the same thickness throughout, about ⅛" (3 mm) thick.

Top Crust: Fold the dough into quarters; using a butter knife, make 3, 1" (2.5 cm) slits (toward the center), 1" (2.5 cm) apart in the folded edges of the dough to allow steam to escape. Unfold the dough so it is in half; place the dough on half of the pie; making sure the edges are covered. The top crust should always be a bit bigger than the bottom. Use scissors to trim the pastry overhang on a pie.

- Glaze the top of your pie with an egg white and water solution before baking to create a glossy, shiny surface. For a sweeter crust, spread milk over the top of the crust and sprinkle with sugar before baking.
- Seal the edge of the pie by tucking the top crust under the bottom crust to keep juices in. Use your fingers to flute the edge, squeezing and pinching.

- If browning too quickly, place wide strips of foil around the edge of the pie.
- Prevent apples from shrinking by cooking them slowly first over low heat for 15 minutes. Add sugar to the apple slices; it will extract some of the juices and make the crust less soggy. Choose more than one variety of apples so that some are sweet and some are tart.
- Pumpkin pie, is best served within a day of baking, because the crust will begin to soften. In season, substitute Fresh Pumpkin Purée (recipe below) for canned pumpkin. If a pie cooks too much, it may crack. Pumpkin pies do not freeze well.

 Fresh Pumpkin Purée: Substitute 1½ cups (375 mL) light cream, or a combination of ¼ cup (60 mL) milk and ¾ cup (175 mL) heavy cream for 1½ cups (375 mL) evaporated milk.

 Pretzel Crust: 1½ cups (375 mL) crushed pretzels, ½ cup (125 mL) sugar and ½ cup (125 mL) butter.

 Granola or Macaroon Crust: 1½ cups (375 mL) crushed cookie, ¼ cup (60 mL) melted butter.

 Graham, Chocolate Wafer, Gingersnap, Vanilla Wafer Crusts: Combine 1¼ cups (300 mL) cookie crumbs, ¼ cup (60 mL) sugar and ¼ cup (60 mL) melted butter. Press into greased pie plate. Bake at 375°F (190°C) for 10 minutes and let cool before filling.

- To make crumbs, place cookies or crackers in a bag and roll them with a rolling pin or process in a food processor.
- **Puff Pastry**: Is a rich pastry prepared by layering pastry dough with bits of butter. When baked, the moisture in the butter creates steam, causing the dough to separate into hundreds of paper-thin, flaky layers.
- **Phyllo (Filo) Dough**: Phyllo (leaf in Greek) is tissue-paper-thin sheets of pastry dough made from flour, water and a bit of oil. Phyllo dough is one of the main ingredients in the Mediterranean specialties baklava and spanakopita.

 Chef's Secret: Homemade pie crust that is too soft should be wrapped in plastic and stored in the fridge for about 15 minutes. Add flour as needed.

 Kitchen Secret: If your pie looks cooked, but the filling is underdone, loosely wrap it in foil and return it to the oven to cook through.

Secrets to Exceptional Cookies

- Make your own colored sugar, it's so easy. Scoop 1-2 tbsp. (15-30 mL) sugar into a plastic sandwich bag. Add a few drops of food coloring, smush them together. Sprinkle colored sugar on cookies. Apply sugar before baking to help sugar stick to dough.
- Take cookies out of the oven a little sooner than the recipe calls for.
- For a puffy cookie, use cold dough and don't flatten before putting cookies into the oven. Add baking soda and a little lemon juice to help cookies rise.
- **Icing Cookies**: Royal Icing is best if you want you to mail cookies; fondant tastes better; use clear vanilla extract if you want a very white icing. A few drops of white food coloring makes it even brighter.
- Nothing beats the flavor and texture of cookies made with real butter! Leave the butter at room temperature so that it mixes easily.
- Use real vanilla to enrich cookie flavor. Not suitable for those with peanut allergies.
- Substitute half the amount of honey for sugar in a chocolate cookie recipe, to create more moist cookies.
- Adding 1 tsp. (5 mL) sour cream to chocolate chip cookie dough creates a chewy cookie.
- To restore moisture to soft cookies that have dried out, wrap a wedge of apple or a slice of bread in waxed paper and put it in the container with the cookies. Remove the apple or bread after 24 hours.
- To create same-sized cookies, use a retractable ice cream scoop, either small, medium or large. Also, if you wet spoons between dropping dough onto pan, the dough will not stick to the spoon.
- Liquid food colors are best for tinting dough in pastel colors. For deeper color, use paste colors, available in cake decorating stores and some kitchen shops. The paste also works best for frostings and glazes since it doesn't thin them. To use paste colors, dip a toothpick into the paste and add it to the icing. Always use a clean toothpick so dough or frosting isn't transferred to the color paste, causing it to mold.
- **Measuring Liquids**: Use a glass-measuring cup; the glass permits you to see the level of the liquid being measured. The cup for liquids should have additional space above the 1 cup (250 mL) line, so that a full cup can be accurately measured without spilling. Check the measurement at eye level.
- **Measuring Dry Ingredients**: Use standard individual cups. Lightly spoon dry ingredients into correct cup size, heap up and level off with edge of spatula by cutting across the top. Use measuring spoons in this way also.

Attention Chocolate Lovers ... Brownie Secrets Revealed!

- Melting butter rather than creaming it with sugar will give you fudge-like brownies. Using plain cake flour will result in tender brownies; all-purpose flour will give a cake-like texture.

- Cake-like brownies contain less butter, more flour and baking powder than do chewier brownies. For chewier brownies, add 1-2 extra eggs.

- Unsweetened chocolate has the highest amount of starch, creating a stiffer brownie. Semisweet chocolate makes a creamier brownie. Combining semisweet with unsweetened, plus 2 tbsp. (30 mL) cocoa gives the best flavor.

- Do not over beat! Stir the ingredients just enough to moisten.

- Use a coated nonstick baking pan instead of glass (over baking is more common when using glass). Use the right size pan according to the recipe.

- Only grease the bottom of the baking pan to allow the batter to rise.

- Do not over bake brownies! Cake-like brownies are done when the sides begin to pull away from the pan or when a toothpick inserted into the center of the brownie comes out clean.

- If using nuts, brown them before adding to the recipe; they will be tastier.

- Brownies are more moist if half of the sugar is substituted with applesauce or sour cream. The brownies will not have a fruity flavor!

- Easy cutting trick. Line the pan with greased parchment paper. When the brownies are baked, remove the brownies along with the paper and cool.

- After the brownies are taken from the oven, score the top of the dessert. Allow brownies to cool completely before cutting. **Note**: Use a plastic knife or table knife for a clean cut. If using a metal knife, cool it in the refrigerator for 20 minutes before cutting.

- Do not refrigerate brownies, doing so will cause them to dry out. If brownies taste a little dried out, reheat them in the oven next to a pan of water.

- To store brownies, place them inside a plastic container or cookie tin. Wrap the inside of the container with plastic or aluminum foil.

- Transporting brownies can be a challenge. When you need to layer them, cover a sheet of waxed paper with a thin layer of butter and place it on top of the brownies before positioning the second layer. This will prevent the brownies from sticking to one another.

Happy Baking!

Better Than an Ordinary Cake

- Shiny pans reflect the heat, and are your best choice for cake baking. Reduce the oven temperature by 25° (10°C) when using glass pans.
- Avoid white residue on a cake by preparing the pan with leftover cake mix instead of flour.
- Cakes are generally categorized by the ratio of fat to flour content. The higher the proportion of fat and sugar to flour, the richer the cake. The proportions of fat and sugar to flour will influence the method of mixing.

 Kitchen Secret: If your cake rose unevenly in the oven you may have a problem with one of the following: The flour (should be the last ingredient added) was not blended sufficiently into the main mixture; the temperature inside the oven was uneven; the oven temperature was too high.

- If cakes tend to crack. Bake longer and on lower heat.

 Kitchen Secret: To make a lighter cake, separate the eggs first. Add the yolks to the butter mixture, beat the egg whites then fold into the batter.

- For a more moist **Carrot Cake**, use 1 cup (250 mL) more of carrots than the recipe calls for. Wrapped airtight, carrot cake will keep at room temperature for up to 2 days or in the freezer for up to 2 weeks.
- **Angel Food Cakes** have no added leavening (such as baking powder), shortening or egg yolks. They are leavened with beaten egg whites and they have a high proportion of egg whites to flour. Angel food cakes make a fabulous no-fat treat.

 Kitchen Secret: For moist homemade cakes, add 1 tsp. (5 mL) vinegar to baking soda in recipe.

- Add double-strength real vanilla to white cakes to enhance the flavor.

 Kitchen Secret: All-purpose flour usually doesn't need to be sifted; stir it lightly with a spoon before measuring. Cake flour does need to be sifted before use.

- If your cake sticks to the pan, return the cake to the oven for 3-4 minutes. Remove from oven and place the pan on a wet towel and wait at least 5 minutes before trying to remove the cake from the pan.
- If parchment or waxed paper sticks to the bottom of a cake, lightly brush the paper with warm water. Let stand 1 minute; remove the paper.
- To avoid lumps in cheesecake, make sure the cream cheese and sugar are thoroughly combined before adding the other ingredients.
- To split layer cakes, loop a long strand of unflavored dental floss around the center of the cake horizontally. Cross the ends and slowly and firmly pull on each end to cut cleanly through the cake.

- To keep a serving plate clean while frosting a cake, place strips of waxed paper 4" (10 cm) wide in a square to cover the edges of the plate. Center the cake on the plate, making sure the strips are positioned to cover the plate on all sides. Frost the cake and then carefully pull away the strips.

- Chill cakes between the filling and the frosting. The cake will be much easier to work with. Apply a thin layer of frosting (known as the crumb coat) to the cake then refrigerate until it is set before applying the final, heavier layer of frosting. This will seal in the crumbs, ensuring a clean final appearance. Dust cakes with cornstarch to prevent icing from slipping.

- When garnishing the sides of a frosted cake with nuts or coconut, it's easy to create a mess. Make handling the cake easier by cutting a cardboard cake round slightly smaller than the cake; place the cake on top of it. Hold the cake over a bowl of chopped nuts or coconut while applying the garnish by hand to the sides of the cake.

- To smooth icing on a cake, dip a metal spatula in warm water before frosting.

- Runny cake icing can be fixed by adding more icing sugar, but you may need a large amount to thicken it. Increase your chances of success by halving the icing and adding icing sugar to only 1 portion.

 Kitchen Secret: Add a pinch of bicarbonate of soda to your icing and the icing will stay moist and prevent cracking.

 Chef's Secret: For a decorative effect on a chocolate cake, place a paper doily on top of the cake and sprinkle with icing sugar. Carefully remove doily.

- Professionally decorated cakes always seem to have a molten, silky look. To get that same appearance in your homemade cakes, frost the sides and top of the cake and smooth out with a spatula as usual. Use a hair dryer to "blow-dry" the frosted surfaces of the cake. The slight melting of the frosting gives it that smooth, lustrous appearance.

- Don't fret if your cake falls apart, instead, celebrate the birth of your "trifle." Layer the cake pieces in a clear bowl with vanilla or chocolate pudding and whipped cream. Top with fruit or chocolate shavings.

 Kitchen Secret: When making meringue, make sure that egg whites are at room temperature before using.

- Before giving up on over whipped cream, fold in a few spoonfuls of additional unwhipped cream. If all else fails, serve it as fresh homemade butter on bread or pancakes. Whipped cream is less likely to separate when a touch of unflavored gelatin is added to the mixture. Icing sugar contains cornstarch, so it also helps to stabilize whipped cream.

- Icing in a can will go twice as far when whipped.

Solutions 2

Index

CENTAX BOOKS MAKE GREAT GIFTS

Household Solutions 1 with Substitutions _____ x $14.95 = $ _____

Household Solutions 2 with Kitchen Secrets _____ x $14.95 = $ _____

FLAVOURS: The Cookbook _____ x $24.95 = $ _____

Grandma's Best _____ x $21.95 = $ _____

Grandma's Kitchen _____ x $21.95 = $ _____

Grandma's Soups & Salads_____ x $21.95 = $ _____

Grandma's Touch _____ x $21.95 = $ _____

Let's Go Dutch _____ x $21.95 = $ _____

201 Fat-Burning Recipes _____ x $19.95 = $ _____

201 MORE Fat-Burning Recipes _____ x $19.95 = $ _____

Create Your Own – Brides Cookbook_____ x $12.95 = $ _____

Create Your Own – Recipes By Me Cookbook _____ x $12.95 = $ _____

Shipping and handling charge (total order) _____ = $ ___5.00___

Subtotal _____ = $ _____

In Canada add 6% GST _____ = $ _____

Total enclosed _____ = $ _____

U.S. and international orders payable in U.S. funds. Prices subject to change.

NAME: _____

STREET: _____

CITY: _____ PROV./STATE _____

COUNTRY: _____ POSTAL CODE/ZIP: _____

❑ CHEQUE *OR* Charge to   ❑ VISA   ❑ MASTERCARD

Account Number:_____

Expiry Date: _____ /_____

Telephone (in case we have a question about your order): _____

Make cheque or money order payable

TO: **Centax Books & Distribution**   **OR**   Order by phone, fax or email:
   1150 Eighth Avenue   **Phone: 1-800-667-5595**
   Regina, Saskatchewan   **FAX: 1-800-823-6829**
   Canada S4R 1C9   **E-mail: centax@printwest.com**

See our website for our complete range of cookbooks,
gardening books, history books, etc.

www.centaxbooks.com

For fund-raising or volume purchases, contact Centax Books & Distribution for volume rates.
Please allow 2-3 weeks for delivery.

CENTAX COOKBOOKS MAKE GREAT GIFTS

REVISED ...

HOUSEHOLD SOLUTIONS 1 WITH SUBSTITUTIONS – 1500 Quick Fixes
by Reena Nerbas

More than the average household solutions book! Solutions to almost every imaginable family concern, from cleaning and reducing chemicals in the home to ingredient and product substitutions, from stain and odor removal to etiquette and table setting, from gardening to energy conservation, from food storage and safety to birthday parties and gift wrapping, from camping tips to choosing wines. This comprehensive, helpful and entertaining book is the perfect newlywed, housewarming, birthday, Christmas and every occasion gift. Plus over 500 substitutions.

Retail $14.95   6" x 9"
176 pages   over 50 line drawings
ISBN 13: 978-1-897010-38-9   perfect bound

NEW RELEASE ...

FLAVOURS – THE COOKBOOK
Sophisticated, Delicious, Elegant
– These three words are what every chef strives for when making a meal. It takes years of practice with different ingredients to deliver true culinary artistry on the plate. If you've ever wondered how they do it, find out now in *Flavours – The Cookbook*.
Learn the tips and tricks to preparing gourmet meals from your very own kitchen. Discover the methods and techniques that can elevate your cooking from the simple to the sublime, all in one book. The flavours of many of these superb recipes are further enhanced by the use of wines, liqueurs, liquors and beer in their preparation. Cooking with spirits can add surprising depth and sparkle to recipes – *Flavours* will show you how.
Since 2003, *Flavours* magazine has delivered hundreds of mouthwatering recipes and stunning food photography from across Western Canada – now you can own the very best of these in *Flavours The Cookbook*.

Retail $24.95   7" x 10"
208 pages   colour photographs throughout
ISBN 978-1-897010-36-5   perfect bound

CREATE YOU OWN COOKBOOKS

MY HOLIDAY RECIPES & TRADITIONS
ISBN 1-894022-55-6

RECIPES BY ME & OTHER SPECIAL PEOPLE
ISBN 1-894022-44-0

BRIDE'S COOKBOOK
ISBN 1-894022-46-7

Create Your Own Cookbooks – each includes a roasting chart, herb and spice chart, ingredient substitutions, ingredient equivalent measures, metric conversion tables, kitchen tips and household hints.
EACH *Create Your Own Cookbook* – Retails for $12.95, 6" x 9", has 144 pages with illustrations throughout and lay-flat coil binding.

GRANDMA'S BEST – Traditional Treats – over 400,000 sold in series
by Irene Hrechuk and Verna Zasada

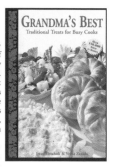

Grandma's Best and *Grandma's Touch* represent the rich multicultural aspect of Canadian life and include treasured family recipes from many cultural groups. A special children's section has recipes that children love and love to make. This satisfying collection of grandma's favorite recipes will please everyone from grandkids to grandads. Here are the satisfying, comforting aromas and flavors that you remember from Grandma's kitchen.

Retail $21.95   7" x 10"
208 pages   10 colour photographs
ISBN 1-894022-66-1   perfect bound
ISBN 13: 978-1-89402-66-8

GRANDMA'S KITCHEN – Comfort Cooking from Canadian Grandmas – over 400,000 sold in series
by Irene Hrechuk and Verna Zasada

Grandma's Kitchen celebrates Canadian cooking as traditional favorites from many other countries become new Canadian traditions. Grandma's Kitchen evokes memories of delicious flavors and aromas. With this cookbook you can prepare your special childhood favorites as grandma used to make them. You can also prepare some of the fabulous recipes made by your friends' grandmas.

Retail $21.95   7" x 10"
208 pages   10 colour photographs
ISBN 1-894022-86-6   perfect bound
ISBN 13: 978-1-894022-86-6

GRANDMA'S SOUPS & SALADS with Biscuits & Breads – over 400,000 sold in series
by Irene Hrechuk and Verna Zasada

Over 100 superb soups and stews range from elegant chilled to hearty vegetable, seafood and meat. Over 70 fabulous salads include fruit, grains, pasta, vegetable and tossed salads. There are also over 25 satisfying yeast and quick breads. Outstanding variation suggestions effectively double the number of soup, salad and bread recipes. These are family-style recipes – grandma's comfort food.

Retail $21.95   7" x 10"
208 pages   10 colour photographs
ISBN 1-897010-02-8   perfect bound
ISBN 13: 1-978-897010-02-0

GRANDMA'S TOUCH – A Canadian Classic – over 400,000 sold in series
by Irene Hrechuk and Verna Zasada

Enjoy your special childhood favorites as Grandma used to make them, updated for today's busy, health-conscious cooks. Enjoy your favorite comfort food from your British, Chinese, French, German, Italian, Irish, Mexican, Russian, Scandinavian and Ukrainian grandmothers. These recipes, using readily available ingredients, are economical, easy to prepare and will delight beginner and experienced cooks.

Retail $21.95   7" x 10"
208 pages   10 colour photographs
ISBN 1-895292-62-9   perfect bound
ISBN 13: 978-1-894022-86-6